A SEASON IN BAGHDAD

(Confessions of a Combat Chaplain)

by

Ernie Carroll

Chp (MAJ) Ernie Carroll
Psalm 91
God Bless!

Nathan
Carroll
Hebrews 11:1

Disclaimer: I have relied on memory, instant messages, emails, cards, video tapes, telephone conversations and letters to reconstruct the events that took place in this book.

Some conversations by me and others in the book are not necessarily word for word accounts of some events, but are based on my recounting of those conversations. To the best of my knowledge they are accurate. Because of the difference in time zones it is also possible that some events may not correspond with the date(s) given.

ISBN/EAN13: 1434898822/9781434898821

Edited by Holly Smith
Ivy Alexander

Photographs by
Ernie Carroll
Jack Bains - Southern Exposure Photograhy
David Wilson - Blount Photographic

Foreword by Ernie Carroll

Cover Design by Nathan Carroll

Typing of Manuscript by Erin Carroll

Text Design and Composition by Lesli Bass

Dedicated To

My Father, Clifford M. Carroll, Jr.
For whom I have a deeper love and understanding
And
My Mother, Margaret Nell Carroll
For whom I hoped to tell our family's story

Contents

Foreword

My name is Ernie Carroll. I am the Director of Missions for the Friendship Baptist Association in Oneonta, Alabama. I was also a chaplain (major) in the Alabama National Guard for almost 15 years. Activated on January 2, 2004, I spent 16 months on active duty and was in Baghdad, Iraq, for one year. While in Baghdad, my son, Nathan, played football and ended up winning a state 3A football championship. Out of that championship and against the backdrop of the ongoing Battle of Baghdad, I began writing a journal. This book is taken from those journal entries. It is the story of a war that separated a father and a son and the love of God, country, and family that caused them to make the choices they did.

In the fall of 2003, my son Nathan's football season had ended. We were looking forward to the following football season, his last, when I was contacted by my National Guard unit and given a phone number to call at the State Military Department in Montgomery, Alabama. I was being transferred to the 731st Maintenance Battalion in Tallassee, Alabama, because they were about to deploy and needed a chaplain. I was placed on alert status with that unit. The President of the United States was about to invade Iraq. The unit I was transferred to was to be part of the northern invasion. I spent several weekend drills preparing for this deployment and my family attended a Family Support Group meeting to prepare them for the upcoming mobilization.

My Guard unit began to practice for chemical warfare by putting on our chemical suits as fast as we could and staying in them for over an hour. We packed crates with most of the essential equipment we would need overseas. When Turkey voted not to allow the U.S. to use their country as a staging area for the invasion, our deployment was delayed and eventually cancelled. I stayed on alert through July and was then able to transfer back to my old battalion, the 231st Chemical Battalion in Oneonta, Alabama. By then I thought I had dodged the deployment bullet.

As a chaplain in the National Guard, I usually led two worship services at weekend drills. Annual training was conducted for two weeks each year where I would conduct worship services in the field for the soldiers. I would also make sure that a visiting chaplain was available to the other units that were in the battalion. These other units were located in places like Moulton, Haleyville, Tuscumbia, and Sheffield near Florence, Alabama. I did a great deal of counseling with soldiers, visiting hospitals, and conducting military funerals as well.

It was in the summer of 1991 that I received my induction into military training at Fort Monmouth, New Jersey. The purpose of the Chaplain Officer Basic Course (CHOBC) was to give chaplains new to the military an induction into military life. Some of the chaplains in my class were prior military, so they knew a lot of the ropes already. We only received a three-day taste of boot camp at Fort Dix, New Jersey. When we went out to the obstacle course our instructor warned us, "Now chaplains, if you see something you can't do, don't try it because you're not 18 any more." This warning was received seriously because one of the chaplains had broken both his arms when he tried to climb down a single rope which appeared to be hanging down three stories!

After CHOBC, I still had to conduct training in the Guard as well. Sustainment Training involves a lot of correspondence work that usually takes about a year to complete. I did not enjoy it. I attended all the officers meetings conducted in our unit and took the PT test every year along with the other soldiers. I would later discover, as my father, a combat veteran, must have known, that no amount of training would prepare me for the fight ahead.

Oneonta's football team enjoyed a great season Nathan's junior year. Oneonta beat Colbert County 15 to 0 in the fourth round of the playoffs to advance to the championship game. This win earned the Redskins a spot in the state championship against Pike County. However, a few days before the 2003 State Championship game between Oneonta and Pike County, I received a phone call from my Guard unit in Oneonta telling me I was being transferred to the 231 Military Police Battalion in Prattville, Alabama, for deployment to Iraq. I was beyond the alert status. There was no way that I was going to tell my children, Erin or Nathan, at a time like that, so I decided to wait until after the game. Unfortunately, thanks to an amazing quarterback, Pike County went on to beat Oneonta 30 to 7.

I knew I had to tell Nathan and Erin I was being activated. Coming off the loss of the state championship football game, Nathan cried as he realized that I would be gone for his senior year, his last year of football. After I told him, I spent a lot of time reflecting over the fact that I was being activated and cried because I wouldn't be there to experience his senior year. I was his biggest fan. I enjoyed the practices as much as the games. His junior year was something to be proud of. He had earned a starting position and maintained it throughout the year. It was as much a challenge for me to keep Nathan ahead of his game by giving him useful tips as it was satisfying for Nathan to be successful on the field. But I knew I had an obligation to fulfill. Nathan would have to trust in the Lord to help him to succeed in football as I would have to trust the Lord to deliver me safely home again. Prayer would be our strategy.

My daughter, Erin, was as equally devastated as Nathan and welled up in tears when I shared the news with her. I remembered her saying, "I just got home from school. Why did you have to tell me this!?" She had just completed her first semester as a college freshman at Samford University. I told her, "There is really no good time to tell you and the sooner the better." Erin then said, "I'm so proud of you, daddy." With that said, I took the rest of the month of December 2003 to get ready to deploy. I had four weeks of vacation left and decided to spend the time with my family and packing for the year ahead.

CHP (MAJ) Steve R. Carroll
231st MP Battalion
Pratville, Alabama
Alabama Army National Guard
Operation Iraqi Freedom II

Chapter One
PRAYER AS STRATEGY

January 9, 2004

I have arrived at Fort Benning. My wife, Renay, has been writing to our prayer partners. She tells them: "I know that you will pray for Ernie and his ministry there. I will not be able to get prayer requests to you as quickly as you might need to know them. I have to trust that God will use your prayers even when you may not know what you need to pray for and apply them in Ernie's situation."

Soldiers are coming to my room for prayer. Held a Bible Study last night and about 20 soldiers came and wanted to share and talk during the study. The Holy Spirit is working in a great way in our time together. I met a soldier that was on medical leave from Baghdad. He described what it is like to be in Baghdad in very vivid detail. He showed us pictures of the Iraqi police station where Aubrey Bell was killed and the vehicle that was used in the bombing.

The days are full and we begin our training early. We study land navigation, mounted land navigation, and how to clear a building. I've even been through the gas chamber! Everyone went through the weapons qualification course, except me. I don't carry a weapon so I wouldn't be doing that. I gather the soldiers on Sunday morning for worship even if we are conducting training in the field.

January 28

Renay and Nathan have come down twice this month. I'm getting to know the soldiers in the unit. Some of them are dealing with divorce and career issues that are causing them problems. Some started a new job right before being called up and didn't have time to learn the new job. Some had to drop out of school and are not able to finish. I pray that all these situations will draw them closer to Christ. Chief Mathews is playing a keyboard. He is a true brother and we pray together daily. Mathews played "My Jesus I Love Thee" and a few other hymns at the chapel service Sunday. It changed the entire atmosphere for worship. We don't have hymn books, but it still made a huge difference for Mathews to play. Many of the soldiers say they are not "religious" but spiritual. When asked what they mean, they say they don't attend church. By January 30th we will have completed deployment certification. Some of the equipment is being readied for shipment overseas, but we don't have a deployment date yet.

February 15

Chris Taylor, one of the soldiers with the 1165th MP Company in Iraq has been killed. The 1165th is an MP company now in Iraq that is a part of the 231st MP Battalion.

February 28

With the military things are constantly changing. All the enlisted soldiers have taken the equipment to a port to be shipped. We are to be deployed at the end of March. My prayer is for Erin and Nathan during this time of transition. Renay and I pray that they will be able to go on with their lives. Erin is nearing the end of her freshman year at Samford University. Nathan starts spring training for his senior year of football and weight training in the summer. This will be hard for Nathan and me. Renay prays that she will become knowledgeable about what an offensive lineman is supposed to do. She also prays for the capture of Osama Bin Laden. She tells me, "I do not know why that request is on my heart so deeply, but I believe that he is behind much of the violence we continue to see in Iraq."

I have seen Renay and Nathan again this week. The attendance at Bible study continues to be good. The soldiers are receptive. I hope that all the soldiers can see The Passion of Christ playing at the theater on base. Renay sends prayer strategy letters to 60 prayer warriors every three weeks.

In a prayer letter that Renay has sent out, she writes:

> Your prayers are being answered. Pray for all of us as we enter "phase two" of this process. I feel like we have somewhat adjusted to Ernie's being at Fort Benning especially since we have been able to see each other on some weekends. Now I feel like we are back at square one when he leaves for Iraq. He has a high calling and I know that God has called him to share Christ with these soldiers in a dangerous place. I know too the safest place to be is in the center of God's will. We covet your prayers for us and for all the soldiers and their families.

March 22

I will be leaving for Iraq in a few days. I will probably spend about two weeks in Kuwait. I have been talking to the chaplain whom I will replace and I will work out of Grace Chapel. I can change the name of the chapel to anything I want, but as I am very traditional, I will keep the same name. There is a main chapel on the base that I will work with some. I know that everyone is joining me in praying for a swift end to this mission. I know I am in the center of God's will by serving my country. Friendship Baptist Association is in good hands. We have a good moderator in Bill Nugent and vice moderator, C.P. Davis. Our secretaries are very supportive. Renay's family has been extremely helpful. They paid for us to stay in a nice motel while Renay, Erin and Nathan visited me at Fort Benning.

March 31

Left Fort Benning on Saturday, March 27. I was able to spend the week with Renay and family before I left. Flew to Frankfurt, Germany, on Saturday night. After a four-hour layover, we flew to Kuwait. Got into Kuwait and spent the night. Ended up flying into the Baghdad International Airport Sunday night. Convoying to our base was an experience. These are the roads where the IEDs are that I have heard so much about. I rode in an armored humvee and Mathews and others rode in an open truck. They all loaded their weapons before we left. It was quite a feeling to be convoying down a road that is a combat zone—the first time ever for me.

Prayed hard all the way. Mathews and I got together when we arrived at our FOB (Ferrin-Huggins) and talked about the perfect peace we had as we traveled down the road. It's all because of the power of prayer. I couldn't help but pray and watch the road for insurgents and think about how I ended up in Iraq to begin with. I wonder what my mother would say about my deployment if she were alive.

I used to travel with my mother to Fort McClellan in Anniston, Alabama, to buy groceries. I remember seeing the new recruits marching down a parade field with their weapons and field gear. I wondered how many were bound for Vietnam. I fully expected that if I had any military experience it would come at the time I graduated from high school. The only time my dad said anything to me about football was the time he told me to keep playing so that I would be in shape if I ever joined the army. In 1972 when I was a senior in high school they held a draft for men born in my birth year. My mother knew my draft number before I did. Because of my dad's condition as a disabled vet she didn't want me to be drafted. She's the one who told me my draft number was too high for me to be drafted—I never was. George, who lived up the street, joined the Navy Reserve and had a six-month tour of duty at sea. I thought since he joined that I would join too, but never did. My greatest ambition at that time was getting out of high school and going to college and earning a degree.

My journey from Oneonta to Baghdad began some time ago when I was at the First Baptist Church of Columbiana, Alabama, attending a senior citizens luncheon with my wife Renay back in the early 80s. Renay was in charge of the event which, among many of the activities, included recognition of those who had served in the armed forces, particularly World War II. I thought then that I couldn't see myself going through the rest of my life not serving my country in the military. I later found out that the National Guard had chaplains from a pastor friend, Tim Williams, who was the pastor at the First Baptist Church Columbiana.

My endorsing agency informed me that I was not qualified to be a chaplain because I lacked the proper Master of Divinity (MDiv) degree. My degree from the Southern Baptist Theological Seminary was the Master of Religious Education (MRE) degree. The MRE degree is a two-year degree instead of the three-year MDiv degree. It took me six years from the time that I felt God was leading me to become a chaplain until the time I was appointed one in the Alabama Army National Guard.

I took additional classes at other seminaries through their extension programs, but felt that I was getting nowhere fast until one day I walked into the office and Renay handed me a letter from Samford University in Birmingham, Alabama. The letter stated that Samford was opening a divinity school. I took the letter in my office and sat down both stunned and excited. God had answered my prayers to get a Master of Divinity Degree and yet be able to keep my ministry position as a Director of Missions with the Tri-Mission Baptist Association. I began my second degree program in seminary.

I graduated from the Beeson Divinity School in May 1990. Shortly thereafter, I waited for my paperwork to go through and was commissioned a First Lieutenant in the Alabama Army National Guard on October 12, 1990. Burney Enzor (state chaplain at the time) remarked on one occasion to a potential recruit that," Carroll just about beat the door down to get in the Guard." I was 36 years old and not 18. Saddam Hussein had invaded Kuwait on August, 2 of 1990 and the U.S. kicked Iraq out of Kuwait on January 16, 1991. I missed Desert Storm, but the next time I wouldn't miss Operation Iraqi Freedom when the U.S. again went to war against Saddam.

I was assigned to the 115th Signal Battalion in Florence, Alabama. I spent nearly 11 years traveling to Florence from Carrollton, Alabama. I remember the first weekend I attended drill. I wore my uniform, but did not know the proper wear. The commander told someone to tell me to put my boot laces inside my boots. There was a lot to learn about the Army.

April 1

Have talked to Renay and Nathan. Nathan is working out every day. The battle is raging in Fallujah. There are several casualties.

April 4

Renay tells me that Nathan has been praying for me—that I will be invisible to the enemy when I go out into Baghdad. She said, "He's been reading too many Civil War books and the Bible, and he knows how to pray." There was a riot in downtown Baghdad today and many Iraqis were killed.

April 7

Had some tea with the Iraqi interpreters. They like to drink tea here. There is a battle still going on in Fallujah. The Marines are saying they have it under control. No more casualties are being reported.

April 9

I was able to talk to my family today. Nathan told me he weighs between 208 and 209. Nathan weighed about 195 last year. A few extra pounds will help him block better. Nathan doesn't take protein supplements to gain weight. We just feed him steak as much as we can. He needs to put on weight to compete—about three more pounds should do it. Then he can see how he handles the other big guys in spring practice. Nathan went to the track three days this week and ran three-fourths of what the other lineman did. I encourage Nathan to run but not to run his weight off.

This was the full unit's first day in Baghdad. The commanders staff, of which I am a part, flew up two weeks earlier than the others in the battalion. The unit convoy narrowly missed an IED that exploded. They had taken a detour around a road where the IED was located.

April 10

In Baghdad, one of the first things I noticed is that this place smells nothing at all like the mountain air that we have in Oneonta. Gone from my sight are the green hills and clear running water of the Locust Fork River that runs through Blount County. Baseball will be on everyone's mind there now, but Nathan is getting ready for spring training. The shoulder and arm brace he uses is worn out.

After the spring training of his sophomore year, Nathan kept talking about his shoulder popping in and out of place. This was the first time I heard anything about a shoulder problem. These incidents became too frequent, and I knew that after spring training something had to be done. When I asked Nathan what exactly happened that created the problem with his shoulder, he said it was when he went out for football in the seventh grade. During a tackling drill his right arm was shoved up and back popping his arm out of place.

The team had two a days at Jacksonville State University. Two days before they started, I took Nathan to a specialist to see about his shoulder. Thankfully, it wasn't serious enough to require surgery—he only needed a shoulder brace. But the brace was too hot for the summer practice sessions. We found one that wouldn't restrict his shoulder movement and was light and cool enough to endure the summer heat. I learned that Nathan has a unique physical trait called "round shoulders." His shoulders tend to slant downward instead of straight across and are thus more prone to popping out. I encouraged him to work on strengthening his shoulders without knowing that he was prone to dislocating them.

We improvised with numerous braces to see what worked best for Nathan. He used a strap for practice that attached to his shoulder pads and then would go around his right arm. When he felt his shoulder move again we put a shoulder cup on top of his shoulder to help absorb impact. This seemed to work well for practice. Nathan would save the shoulder brace for games.

I heard the U.S. is attacking Fallujah again. The insurgents have taken three Japanese hostages and are going to burn them if the Japanese troops don't leave. We need to blast them. Lots of concern about hostage taking now. There are reports of a couple of Americans being captured and now held hostage, but the military isn't commenting. The U.S. offered a ceasefire to Fallujah militants after the U.S. started attacking yesterday. I am planning my first service in Baghdad. I've been away from my work four months.

April 11, Easter Sunday

Some of the units we are replacing got extended for 90 days. The soldiers were very upset. Renay e-mailed a picture of herself, Erin, and Nathan with the Easter Bunny taken at a mall. The Easter Sunrise Service was great. I felt the Holy Spirit at work. What made it so good is that I preached a sunrise service in an ancient biblical land. It was held outside. About 10 people came. More would probably have come if I hadn't planned it at the last minute. We have not officially taken over all responsibility yet. The phones are shut down because a soldier from another unit got killed last night. We were awakened at 1:30 a.m. and told an attack was imminent. Each soldier was given five clips of ammo. Everyone, except me, that is.

We were up until five o'clock waiting for an attack. I gathered everyone around and had prayer. I prayed that we would become invisible to the enemy. The attack never came. Renay said that this is the way Nathan prays. He prays that I become invisible to the enemy. She also tells me that she is praying for my protection. She said, "You are in God's hands, and He is protecting you. There are a band of angels around you to protect and minister to you. You have God's armor on from Ephesians 6." I told her to ask everyone to pray for divine protection. I do feel safe. Nonetheless, pray for protection. Prayer is our strategy for surviving this war.

April 16

A note to Bob Paul: "It is great to hear from you. Please be in prayer for me and my family. Some of the troops were extended and they are taking it hard. Pray for my son Nathan as he starts his senior year of spring football the first week of May. Nathan made all-county second team at left guard. Please remember him in your prayers. I am his personal trainer. —Ernie"

April 20

I got my uniforms today. I have been wearing the same uniform for three weeks. I put my duffel bag with my clothes in it onto a truck that had not yet arrived at my base.

April 21

I turned on the web cam while Renay and I talked. She told me my hair was sticking out in the back like it always does. I told her it's because I was wearing a helmet today. We talked about the new guard unit from Wyoming coming in. Congress started holding the 9/11 hearings. Renay wants to go visit some churches if she can get her schedule under control. She said the owner of the Phillips 66, Mark Jackson, asked her yesterday if she had heard from me. He said he prays for me because I need all the prayers I can get.

I told Erin I saw a mouse in my room this morning. I am going to tape the bottom of the doors tonight.

Renay tells me, "That would be a good idea. I would too. Mice are messy. Put a mouse trap out. Do you want me to send you some?"

I respond, "The mice are our friends. Yes! The flat sticky kind—and lots of them."

Renay comments, "The mice are not our friends unless they can get you home somehow."

"The mice will build me a boat."

" You sound like you need to go to bed?"

"Yes."

"Protect yourself from the mouse."

April 23

Talked about the fact that I still had not received my Easter packages in the mail. Dr. Rick Lance, the Alabama Baptist State Executive Director, was the first person from whom I received a card in the mail. Dr. Lance has been very supportive of my deployment. Our commander's convoy got blasted last night. No one was hurt. No real damage. It happened about 7:30 p.m. our time, 4:30 a.m. at home. Mary Parker was up praying for them at that time. Renay prays for the commander two to three times a day. She prays two to three times a day for every soldier on the roster. She prays that those who are not Christians will become Christians. She prays that those who are will grow, and God will use me in that process.

Renay started telling me about tires that she had put on my pickup truck that I let Nathan drive to school every day. He was proud to drive my truck.

Nathan has weight lifting competition next Monday. He has spring training on Tuesday and Wednesday and gets his football gear today. I want Nathan to send me pictures of the new tires. I wish I were there for the spring training.

Junior Varsity football at Oneonta consists of seventh and eighth graders. A few players played on varsity. Nathan had thought about playing in the seventh grade, but I didn't think he was ready to play that soon. It was in the spring of Nathan's seventh grade year that he finally went out for football. I remember he was very excited about playing. I went to practice and watched him from a set of old bleachers that looked like they were from the old high school when it was located in the middle of Oneonta. I watched Nathan until practice was over and then I drove him home.

When we arrived home that evening and began talking about practice, Nathan was really upset and didn't want to go back the next day. I knew he wasn't use to the pads and all the hitting he would have to do. This was a totally new experience for Nathan. I encouraged him to give it another try the next day and assured him it would only get better. I told him, "If you quit, you'll regret it."

Renay said, "I wish you were here. You don't know how bad. Prayer is our only hope and real possibility. If that is the case, and we believe it is, I and others are praying like never before. I have never prayed like I do now. I pray all during the day and before bed and set my alarm and pray in the middle of the night when I get up. I'm praying constantly. I pray all day long. I'm glad you are too. It is the only way to cope with this."

I had a book that I misplaced. I asked Renay to pray that I would find it. I felt a little discouraged about being in Baghdad. I felt like I was in a huge predicament. Renay tells me, "I know that God has placed you there. God is going to win the war in our life for you in Iraq. That means that whatever His will is for you to be there, He wants to accomplish it because you are willing for that to happen and I am too."

April 24

Nathan asked me about the bomb blast that hit the commander's vehicle. We talked about his weight. They are getting ready for spring practice. He couldn't wait to tell me that he got his pads today. I looked at the tape of last year's football season. There was another soldier that watched it with me. He said most of the touchdowns Oneonta scored are because Oneonta's running backs broke tackles. Nathan said he benched 215 today. He got a total of six by himself and then had help with the other six. I asked Nathan how much he weighs. He tells me 209. I would like to see him gain one more pound. He needs to get to 210. Nathan will be working out all summer.

Oneonta will have 51 guys on the team like last year. They will have 13 seniors and 24 juniors during spring. Nathan also told me that on Wednesday he hang clinged 215. More than he ever has. Nathan's coach, John Niblett, wants him to play right tackle. Coach Niblett wants him to put his right hand down if he is on the right side. Nathan said he can't during a game because his shoulder brace won't let him. I am curious as to why Niblett would want to do that.

Nathan tells me that Coach Niblett told him he wouldn't be putting as much weight on his hand with the new stance they are going to use this year. I am hoping that he will change his mind. Nathan said he wasn't about to argue or question him, so he said, "Yes sir!" I told Nathan to do the best he could and try to adapt. It may have a lot to do with the plays the offense is going to run this year. He is going to be challenged by some folks for playing time. I reminded him, as I always do, to work hardest against the biggest and best defensive player on the team. He's the one you want to block the hardest. Oneonta has some very good linemen. If Nathan can block them, he can block anybody he comes up against in a game.

I have just recently moved into my new room. Renay asked me if I had gotten all my suitcases and everything else we packed to send over. I told her I had.

I told Nathan not to be surprised if Coach Niblett gets one of the bigger linemen to give him competition. Coach Niblett likes to keep the pressure on Nathan. Renay agreed that with 24 juniors, Coach Niblett is really going to try to work them. Renay lets me know that Nathan really appreciates being able to talk to me. She said that Nathan seems to gain more confidence and self-assurance after talking to me. I believe he will be fine. I wondered what Renay had heard on the news. The only thing she said she heard is that Al Sadr is trying to use the bombings in Baghdad that killed Iraqis to blame the U.S. occupation. I wanted to tell her to be sure to tell Nathan to hit hard in tackling drills. This is a point I always try to help Nathan make:

> Get the coach's attention during Oklahoma drills. Try to do such a good job that the coach calls out your name at least one time a day during practice. This is especially true when done during the blocking and tackling drills. A good time for Nathan to do this was during the Oklahoma drills. Oklahoma drills are the drills where players get in two lines on opposite sides of each other and get down in a three point stance with one player blocking for a ball carrier lined up behind the blocker and a defensive tackler lined head up on the blocker that tries to tackle the ball carrier once the whistle blows. This is a drill that separates the players from the scrubs. If you catch the coaches' eyes during these drills you're going to stick in his mind as a player that really likes to put the wood to folks.

I ran today but almost didn't get it in because of a sand storm. These dust storms make you feel like you've never had a bath. "I feel dirty all the time," I tell Renay. "All the time." I asked Nathan if there is anybody else playing right tackle, but he didn't know. I reminded Nathan to drive his feet as I always do:

> Drive your feet harder with each successive play so that you're driving your feet harder as the game goes on. This means that you should be driving your feet harder in the fourth quarter than in the first. Keep driving your feet until the whistle stops blowing. Drive through the goal post on every play. The other player is going to pause at some point in the play and when he does that's when you're going to be able to finish off the block by knocking the defensive lineman to the ground.

Erin then wanted to tell me what some crazy people wrote on the bulletin board by the cafeteria at Samford. She said on the bulletin board there was a sign that said, "In case of fire...Please exit the building." Someone else wrote, "In case of fire, RUN!" She said, "Mom thought that was funny." Then underneath that they have these free newspapers and below that, it said in pen, "So's you's can learn." Erin got a kick out of that one. She told me about a number of people who had been asking about me. Sylvia Odom and Anna Ray, Mary Bellew, Audie Nesmith, and Steve Sellers. "The student ministries people at Samford are praying for you," Erin tells me.

Everyone was moving to new rooms in the headquarters building. Everyone except me. Finally Maj. Compton came and told me they had a room for me in a building next to the headquarters building where I could stay. It's the same building where the chapel annex is located. I would eventually move into this building. When the chaplain I would replace re-deploys, I will move into the room he occupies in the chapel itself.

Had a rocket attack this morning. I was at breakfast at the time. It wasn't as close as it sounded. One of our soldiers was injured by shrapnel from this attack. I went to the Green Zone to see him at the CSH (combat support hospital). He had an injury to his hand.

April 25

I had a good service last night at my worship service. I told Renay we have good chaplains here, especially Chaplain Chip Nicholas.

Nathan was getting ready to go to school and I told him to tell Coach Niblett that I said hello. I tell Renay it's really hard.

"How is it hard?" she asks.

I tell her, "I hope it doesn't turn out to be a huge disappointment for me."

"What would be a disappointment? That you went to Iraq?"

"It would be a big disappointment for me not to see Nathan's football games," I said. "Too bad for me."

"No, Ernie, Nathan understands what you are doing. He told me one day that the fact you are there is a motivation for him. It makes him work harder. I'll try to send you everything I can. I still believe you'll be home soon."

"I just don't get to be one of the Dads on the sidelines. Just pray. It's my only hope."

"Yeah, I know you miss that. I did wonder if I could get a blow-up man with your face on it and sit you up there for Nathan. You know, those big life-size cardboard people you see in the music store."

"When I talk to others about it they can't comprehend it."

"Ernie, we are praying. I woke up at 1:30 a.m. last night before my 2:00 a.m. alarm went off to pray. Then I prayed from 6:00 to 6:30 a.m."

"Good."

We talked more about the election coming up on June 30. There was a lot of discussion about what the make-up of the new government would look like. There is speculation if the new government would have anyone from the present governing council serving.

Renay told me that Nathan had washed the logs on the front porch of our log home. She said, "He is trying so hard to help do things you would do and I paid him for helping." God did a great thing yesterday in your service and He helped me too by speaking to me about it."

"Good," I tell her.

"We just have to pray again today to help it all be better."

"It was great."

"That is why you are there Ernie. Soldiers are lost and some of them could meet God out there in battle. You are there to help them get ready. There is no greater mission or calling than that. The kids and I all know and believe that."

"I feel the people came to the service searching for something and they got filled."

Renay told me about a ladies conference where Erin gave her testimony. Erin told them, "One of my challenges right now is having a dad in Iraq." Crying, she continued, "But his ministry is awesome there and it's where I know he needs to be. And I am at Samford, where I need to be."

Renay said that after it was over, several of the women came up to me and hugged her. One told her, "I don't see how you can be so strong." Renay replied, "I am only strong one day at a time."

I called Renay and told her I had to go over by the airport to the Iraqi Support Group. They had a casualty where they were looking for weapons of mass destruction. They came under small arms fire. There was a small chemical fire inside one of the buildings they were trying to clear. One of the soldiers in E Company was killed. There were two casualties. The soldier from E Company was not directly attached to our unit. We only had administrative control over the company. The commander needed me to go with him in case they needed someone to do a Critical Incident Debrief. CID is used to help the soldiers vent and tell their stories whenever there is a casualty. This keeps the soldier talking about their feelings rather than having things pile up. Renay said that she would be praying for me. "I love you. God is with you. You are in

His hands. You have His full armor on," Renay tells me. When we got to BIAP, I found out that all the arrangements had been made for a memorial service, but I wouldn't have any responsibility in it.

When I got back that night, Renay told me she had heard about it on CNN and Nathan saw it on TV. The soldier in our company that was killed had only been in Iraq for two weeks. He was killed by flying debris. While we were over at BIAP, we got a report that one of our vehicles rolled over. As it turned out, no one was seriously injured. One female soldier had to stay overnight for observation. I went to see her over at the Troop Medical Clinic when I got back to our FOB, I had prayer for her. Renay wrote the following thought about last nights service.

> In Baghdad tonight
>
> In Baghdad tonight there is the Great I Am,
> He is offering salvation, hope, and peace in Baghdad tonight.
>
> As God's faithful servants proclaim the one true God,
> There is salvation in Baghdad tonight.
>
> In Baghdad tonight—God's servants continue their toil,
> While the faithful back home pray.
> As we lift holy hands to the
> Great I Am.
> There is comfort and peace in Baghdad tonight.
>
> In America today—
> Are soldiers and families in grief and mourning,
> Loved ones lost through the ultimate sacrifice,
> To the separation of loved ones in battle.
>
> In Baghdad tonight,
> The battle rages,
> Over the hearts and minds of
> Soldiers and Iraqis tonight.
>
> May the Great I Am come and help us,
> Have mercy on us,
> And may peace come to the hearts and minds—in Baghdad tonight.

April 29

Nathan did good in football yesterday; he seems to have picked up where he left off, Renay tells me.

I ask her, "What makes you say that?"

"I was out there from 5:00 to 7:00 p.m. watching him. He started out at right tackle. I'm not sure he would know what to do, but he seemed to and he said he did."

"Great. How does the team look?"

"The team looks great and the second team looks strong too. The first string kind of clicks like it did last year."

I asked her about one of the big guys on the team that played behind Nathan on offense. Nathan had to go up against him in practice. Nathan blocked him a good bit. This meant that Nathan did a good job if he was blocking someone as big as that particular lineman. Nathan was able to drive his feet and get good movement on him. I'd be worried if he didn't.

Nathan really wants to talk to me about football, but it's night for me and the morning for him. So, I have to wait for him to get up. Coach Niblett asked him to pray the first prayer of spring practice. He prayed for the troops and then he prayed, "God if it be Your will, let us win the state championship this year." He was so proud that Coach Niblett asked him to pray and he laid the goal right out there in God's hand.

I asked about Nick Ratliff and how he's doing. Nick is one of the best linemen on the team. One of the kids Nathan blocked swung his helmet at Nathan after a play. Nathan stood his ground against him and told him, "Don't start anything." In the locker room the kid came up to him and said, "Hey, I'm sorry Nathan. I shouldn't have done that. I was wrong." Renay told Nathan, "Maybe we'll have a better team with attitudes like that."

After we attended the memorial service of the soldiers killed in the chemical plant accident and returned that afternoon, our commander went back out. That's when he got IED'd. The one vehicle I had been traveling in did not receive any damage. The soldiers in the other vehicles found out that I had prayed for protection of that vehicle and they let me know they wanted prayer as well the next time we went out. The soldiers drive crazy, but they have to. It increases survival. When I told Renay this she said, "I pray over the humvee you ride in, any place you step your foot, and any place you lay your head."

Renay tells me Nathan's up and I ask him about a lot of the players on the team and the positions they play. We talk a good deal about this. Later, Renay told me Coach Niblett had made a note at the bottom of the permission slip he sent home which said that the student would have to turn in his equipment if his parent complained about their child's playing time. Coach Niblett told parents that he was chewed out by several parents and wasn't going to put up with it this year. Some of the parents are strong-minded and this could be a potential problem. I told Renay how much I wished I could be there for the season. She tells me, "I know you do. I know football is hard. I'm just glad that you got to see him play last year and do so well. We are trusting that this year will be no different."

May 2

Preached at the Main Chapel this morning. There were about 100 soldiers present. They were from places like Oregon, Wisconsin, and California. I preached by flashlight because the power was off at my chapel tonight. Had about 25 present.

May 5

Nathan and I talked a little about spring practice. He is having trouble blocking one of the defensive tackles on the team. The DL was getting away from Nathan by cutting to the right and then left. Nathan was open to suggestions. The field was a little muddy from all the rain they were having so everyone was slipping some. The DL is fast and cuts before Nathan can latch on. Nathan tells me he did a good job of driving his feet, keeping his head up, and his rear end down. Keeping his head up is the number one rule we have about football. I always tell Nathan to keep your head up and your rear end down. Safety always comes first.

I tell him he would learn his opponent's tendencies and that he has one of the best defensive linemen in 3A football on his team. "Anticipate a little," I tell him. "Coach Niblett tells him every day he did well since you aren't here to do it," Renay reminds me.

May 6

I talked to Nathan for a minute and then told him I would have to get off the computer because a soldier had been killed. All soldiers are required to shut down computers when the death of a soldier from our FOB (forward operating base) occurs. This prevents news of the death getting out before family members are notified. It is his birthday so I wanted him to go ahead and open up his presents that I sent him so I could watch him on the web cam. Nathan had a good day of practice yesterday. I had to hurry him up because soldiers were looking over my shoulder waiting to shut computers down. I bought him a watch from one of the Iraqi interpreters and CDs and DVDs. I told him happy birthday and he thanked me for the presents.

May 12

Nathan had another good day of practice. I wondered if he just was saying that or if he really did. When I ask him, he tells me he really did. Renay told me later that he had a good practice. I had told Nathan the day before that he needed to watch the defensive tackle's waist so that when he juked, Nathan could keep him in his sights. The defensive tackle may try to put a swim move on Nathan and at least his waist can't twist and turn and move as fast as the tackle's arms and legs might. Nathan said that he did everything he could legally to keep his man from getting to the ball. He focused on the tackle's waist and that helped him a lot. My best advice to Nathan was, "Sometimes you just have to get it in your head that you're going to block your man and see yourself doing it." Nathan has FCA (Fellowship of Christian Athletes) this morning and his scripture verse is Matthew 21:22, "Whatever you ask for, believing in prayer, you will receive." Renay said that Nathan is believing I'll come home. The spring jamboree game is coming up and I told Renay that I hoped she could get me a tape of the game.

Nathan got into the Math Honor Society at school which is a big deal at Oneonta. His math ability doesn't come from me, so it must be from his mother's side. Nathan had struggled with math when he was younger.

I just got on the Internet with Renay, but had to get off. A soldier had been killed.

May 16

Started talking to Renay on the Internet, but I had to get off. "What happened?" she asks me.

"Will be right back," I reply hesitantly.

"Are you there?"

"We are being attacked. It's a mortar attack. Incoming."

"Are you okay!? Are they attacking the base!?"

"I have to get my body armor on," I tell her.

The conversation ends.

May 17

Renay asked me if there were any more mortar attacks, which there had been. The news was talking about troops coming from South Korea. I think this is a good idea. It could only help the situation. This is about the time the prison abuse scandal is breaking out in Iraq.

May 18

I just got back from the Green Zone. A gunner in a humvee was wounded by an IED attack. The humvee was passing under a walkway bridge that went across the highway, and as it passed by, it exploded. The insurgents set them up so that the force of the explosion is downward into the gunner on top of the humvee. The gunner's injury wasn't life threatening but serious enough that he would be sent to Germany for more surgery. Renay tells me, "I wish I had known you were out there; I can pray in the night if I know you are out there riding around in the badlands." They have found a rocket with nerve gas in it. Now we are having to walk around with our gas masks.

I wanted to hear about the football news since Oneonta had just finished playing the spring game. Nathan played at right tackle which was new for him during spring training. Nathan told me that the team has studied the game film. Coach Niblett said that the right side of the line had done a good job. He made that comment twice during the film study. Overall, Nathan did a good job. We know that everyone makes mistakes and Nathan was no exception. This is the time of the year when you don't mind making mistakes because you have time to correct them.

Renay told me to read 2 Kings Chapter 6. She said, "Verses 14 through 16 talk about angels guarding the mountain and God opened the eyes of the young man to see them." A lot of people do need their eyes opened up to see the Lord at work all around.

May 19

Talked to Erin a lot about her major at Samford University. She's in vocal performance right now. May change to a music minor.

May 20

Renay bought and sent me another desert tan uniform. I got it today. This is the 142nd day of activation. I am very thankful for those who are praying for me and my family. Constantly being interrupted by mortar attacks while e-mailing and talking on the phone. You gain a new perspective on life when you sit at breakfast and hear the sound of bombs coming from the opposite direction than they came from last week and a different part of the building is shaking this week. Harold Jennings is coming by the house back home to spray for wasps. He's glad to help out while I'm gone. Mary Bellew called and said that they are getting together a lot of stuff to send to the soldiers.

Renay said that she lays in the bed every night waiting for the phone to ring or the computer to buzz. "Whatever you need on your end to communicate, you need to have it. I have sent phone cards to use. I don't care if you wake me up. I don't do anything around here but wait for you to get home anyway and things to keep me busy. Like buy food and pay our taxes."

"I was two minutes away from being hit by a mortar the other day."

"What happened?" Renay asked nervously.

"I had walked through the gate in back of our headquarters building to go around the front to head to my building. I passed in front of our headquarters building and was walking toward the patio area of my building to go inside when a mortar hit. The concussion was hard."

"What time of the day was it?"

"It was in the evening almost dark."

I found out the next day that a mortar had landed on top of the roof while CPT. Lake was up there talking to his wife. He wasn't hurt but the folks that were with him practically jumped off the roof of the building. That really put a stop to my going out at night. Now I try to be in before dark.

Nathan and I start talking and I ask him about Coach Niblett. Nathan said that Coach Niblett was doing fine. Nathan ate three steaks the night before and I asked him how much he weighed. He told me 205. He lost about five pounds during spring practice.

May 30

Renay had a dream that I came home. "You literally came home for the night," she said. "You were here! You drove home with two friends and we put them up for the night. I just kept saying, 'I can't believe you did this.' Then you knocked on the computer and I woke up."

Our church is getting a new Minister of Youth. Nathan is going to play drums in the 8:30 a.m. worship service. Our vice moderator is starting a new church so they are going to petition our association for membership.

I haven't seen Nathan's football tape yet. I told Sgt. Major Lee that the TV and VCR is the recreation building is broken. He said that he is going to get it fixed.

There was a car bomb in Baghdad today. There is a lot of talk on the news about the new interim government in Iraq and its relationship with the U.S.

May 31

Today we had a Memorial Day ceremony. I had the invocation and Mathews had the benediction. It was short, but good. I told Renay to tell Nathan that I have been watching some of the spring training game. I think the team looks sluggish.

Last night a soldier was killed, so the Internet is down. I preached on Habakkuk. I got my signs for the chapel that I have put up on the wall in front of the headquarters building, the front of my building, and above the chapel door. We have new chairs in the chapel. It feels more reverent in our chapel now. It really looks nice. I told Mathews that as a Christian in full-time ministry, prayer had always been an important part of my life, but not like it is now. Prayer should occupy a large part of what we do each day. Praying on the hour helps.

Oneonta lost to St. Clair County High School and Tarrant High School. Things look bleak. The team was upset about the loss. Brody Cornelius was hurt on the last play of the St. Clair County game. Everybody wonders if they can make it to state playoffs.

June 1

Iraq has a new interim president who says he wants the U.S. out of Iraq soon. I talked to Mathews a lot about it today. There is a soldier over at the CSH that I need to go see soon and I need to get ready for my Bible study tomorrow. A great many of the churches in our association back home are sending care packages to all our troops. Renay is excited that the churches are going out of their way for the soldiers. Shannon O'Neal, the new pastor at First Baptist Blountsville, and his wife, along with Jeanette Statham, our Association WMU Director, have outdone themselves to help send care packages. The soldiers appreciate everything that is being sent to them. The days can get really long here. I just try to stay busy studying and preparing for Bible studies and sermons. I strive to share the love of Jesus with those around me. Renay says I should point them to Christ. "But can you sense God using you where you are?" she asked me one day. I told her that I did.

June 2

I sent Renay some pictures of me visiting a wounded soldier at the CSH so that she could put them in our associational newsletter. I went with CPT Davis in a convoy to visit this soldier, then I had to hitch a ride to get to the hospital. Afterwards we went to an Iraqi police station for them to conduct their mission.

I overheard on the radio chat that there were three Iraqi bodies at the police station. When we got there I walked through the gate of the station and saw from a distance what appeared to be bodies lying on the back of a pickup truck. I walked over to the bodies and saw the remains of figures that you could no longer identify. The bodies had been ripped apart by bullets. Flies covered up the corpses. One of the men that had been killed had his jaw completely shot off and all you could see was the upper roof of his mouth. Another body had its guts shot and hanging out. It was an awful site to say the least.

Had Bible study tonight. It was about perseverance in prayer. The crowd wasn't very big but those that did come enjoyed it.

June 3

Wondering if the elections in Blount County are being held today. I am getting ready for a sermon for Sunday. I need to ask Renay to send me a commentary when I talk to her. Have been busy talking to a soldier. I have counseled two soldiers this week from the same unit.

June 4

I wish I could hear some news of other countries sending troops. Counseled another soldier today. Ran about a mile. No mortar attacks. It seems too quiet. Have been able to send a few pictures over e-mail. Finished watching an Oneonta scrimmage tape.

June 5

It has been quiet here on the FOB the last few days. Have been getting a sermon ready. Talked awhile to Renay, Erin, and Nathan. Played pool and went to a staff meeting.

We received an intelligence briefing about some insurgents setting up a mortar tube for an attack. Somehow when they set it up they must have leaned over the firing tube and the mortar exploded and killed all of them. You could hear some people saying, "Ohhh, that's good stuff."

June 6

I have to put lotion on the bottom of my feet because they are dry and cracking. The hot weather has baked them. The heat of the ground oozes into them making cracks the size of the Grand Canyon.

June 7

I do a lot of preaching, but I don't get the feedback that Renay gives me. I'm not saying that people don't appreciate it, but it's not the same thing as having your biggest supporter here to see what you do. Every day here is so huge. Felt like I did preach a good sermon yesterday. Cleaned up my room a little today. The news said that Rumsfield went to Bangladesh to try to get them to send troops to Iraq.

Four MPs (military police) from one of the other battalions were killed and I will attend the memorial service. Two were killed on one day and the other two the next. Someone made a decision to send those soldiers down the same hot route the very next day. The commander made mention of this to me. At least our commander puts the safety of our soldiers first.

Renay asked me about a couple of football camps that she wants Nathan to attend. He will be on choir tour during one of them and the other one is at

Mountain Brook High on July 2nd. Two-a-days in July won't be as bad as the week-long one. I would hate for Nathan to get hurt right before two-a-days start. I keep remembering when Zac Miller got his jaw broken at a training camp at Samford University. He had to have surgery on his jaw and missed the first two games of the season.

Renay tells me, "This is one more decision I have to make. It helps having someone give an opinion to make decisions. I feel like I'm having to make every single decision around here. Every little thing, I have to think, 'okay, how am I going to handle this one?'"

June 9

I talked more about the classes Erin is taking at Samford. Getting ready for Bible study tonight. Nathan is going back to his old position at left guard. This will give Oneonta more power running the ball and make the running game more punishing.

June 10

I just got back from a memorial service for four National Guard soldiers. There's not that much to say. It was just sad. Renay wanted to know what the service was like. The pertinent question: "Did it honor the soldiers?" I told Renay there's not a good way to do it, but under the circumstances it was good. I just try to show up and give support.

"Ernie, you are doing more than that for the soldiers there." she tells me. "Without guys like you what hope do soldiers like that have? You are the only message of hope they have. I pray for those in your unit who aren't Christians at least two times a day."

The chaplain's message was brief. One thing I learned about these memorial services is that the Army likes to keep them short. The services are for the soldiers to remember their fallen comrades in a combat zone. Each fallen soldier is usually given the Bronze Star Medal which is placed along side the M-16 rifle that is turned upside down and a helmet placed on top of the weapon. A picture of the soldier and a pair of the soldier's boots are all placed on a three-step box painted black called a "stairway to heaven." Usually the battalion commander, the company commander, and at least two of the soldier's friends pay tribute to the soldier with words of remembrance and respect. This helps the soldiers in their grieving process and helps them to focus on the mission. All the chaplains in the brigade attend memorial services for any soldiers killed within that brigade. As a chaplain, I attend the services as a part of the commander's staff. At home, the funerals you attend for the most part are for people who have lived long, enriched lives. The people here that are killed are so young. The ages of the soldiers killed range from 24 to 52. They were very young and had full lives ahead of them. War is so terrible. Many of the people here do seek God, but others want to ignore Him. They deny their own mortality.

Renay asks, "We see that here don't we? It's everywhere." "I understand more of what Jesus must have felt like," I tell her. She sees it as identifying with the sufferings of Christ as He looks out over a lost world of people who won't come to Him. Renay prays:

> Father, there is so much pain and hurt where Ernie is. If I were lost in this situation I would want Jesus. He hurts even though he does not know these soldiers, but he identifies with them. Father, please come to Ernie and fill the room where he is right now. Let him know Your presence by faith. Let him sense the angels that are in the very room where he is. Protect him and minister to his needs right now just as you did Elijah when he was so sad and lonely. Father, we need You. We need to hear a word from You as to how Ernie can go on with this and for how long he has to go through with this. We know You are there, breathing Your Holy Spirit in him. Help him, Lord. Heal his hurt and trauma, Lord. Only You can do this. In Jesus' name, Amen.

Renay really encouraged me to get some "Ernie" time. Get distance from what I had just been through, which usually comes from playing pool. "You are being traumatized every time you go through something like this," she reminds me.

Attending a memorial service usually involves a trip outside our base. It means you have to travel in a convoy out on the roads which, in Baghdad, are the front lines. On the way over to the service we had to take a small detour because an IED (improvised explosive device) was discovered and tanks were blocking the road. The detour took us closer to houses that were just beyond the main road. All of a sudden there was a loud explosion and my driver yelled out "YOW! Get out of here!" Within a few seconds, though, we realized they had detonated the IED, but it scared us nonetheless. Our driver held her composure. No profanity.

I looked at more of Nathan's spring game film. It didn't look too promising, even though there were a few bright spots. I think Coach Niblett was playing it close to the vest and didn't want to show that much. That's one reason why he played a small player at the nose tackle position. Up the middle is where most of Oneonta's opponents were making their yardage. I prayed that Coach Niblett would get a hold of this before the season began. The Redskins have a lot of work to do before the season gets under way. Nathan still did a good job. He needs a little more killer instinct though. Yesterday, Coach Niblett complimented Nathan on his workout. He kidded around with him by saying, "I'm going to make you a wide out, Carroll!—You know I'm just kidding." I'm under the impression that Nathan needs to move back to left guard to give Oneonta more power in the running game. That's exactly what Coach Niblett has already done.

Coach Niblett and Karon, his wife, sent me an encouraging e-mail:

> We recently got your e-mail address from Renay and wanted to let you know that you are in our prayers. We are praying for God's protection and that you will be back in Oneonta for Nathan's senior season as a Redskin. It won't be the same in the stands without you. Joshua 1:9

We exchanged two brief e-mails and I wrote back the next day:

> I am glad that Nathan got to move back to left guard. He is left-handed, so he may feel more comfortable on the left side of the line. I'm sitting here in my body armor because we heard an explosion outside. This is crazy. Please continue to pray.

Many times I would have to talk to Nathan about the tough days he had at practice when he felt like he wasn't doing his best. The most effective way to encourage Nathan was to attend practice. I felt this made the statement to Nathan that I care about what you do and the activities in which you are involved. My own dad never saw me play in any football games while I was on the B-team at Woodlawn High School. Having a viable interest in Nathan's extra curricular activities was important to Nathan. If I was not at practice, he was just as anxious to fill me in on what took place, as I was to hear what he had to say. While a lot of parents quit showing up at practice as the season progressed, I was always there. To avoid distracting the team, I would park up on the hill behind the press box at the stadium and watch practice from that vantage point.

Of course, there were days when Nathan did not do so well and those days were usually on Mondays. I would try to listen and then focus on the area where I thought he could improve. When I went to his practices his junior year I would always meet him at his car and comment on practice. I would compliment him and make at least one suggestion as to what would help him have a better practice. By the time Nathan was a junior, I usually only needed to make only one key suggestion for him to look at because he was getting it "down pat."

The first few days in pads were always tough for Nathan, whether at the beginning of spring practice or the beginning of fall practice. It took Nathan about three days to get back into the swing of things. I often would try to demonstrate what blocking should be like until he got back into the routine and understood what Coach Niblett was trying to teach him. I would pick Nathan up after practice and head home to go over a few details. We would get on our driveway and have our own skull session by walking through his blocking schemes. The bad part of this is that it required a little live action on my part so that Nathan could get the right effect. We would practice his firing off the ball into his opponent or getting his head on, the right or left side of the defensive tackle depending on which gap the ball carrier would run through. I would show Nathan how to fire off the ball and place his helmet on the defensive tackle's numbers and work his head to either side of the opponent. We played a little smash-mouth football in order to remind Nathan of some basic blocking techniques he had laid by the wayside during the off season and bring him up to speed.

I do remember that I got some nice bruises on my arms because of this. One year I had an early spring annual training with the National Guard in April and still had the bruises on my arm because of those practice sessions. Nathan was in spring training at the time. I remember pointing them out in a sermon to the soldiers who were gathered for worship that Sunday morning at Camp McClellan near Anniston, Alabama. I talked about the fact that I was willing to bear the bruises for my son if I thought it would help him improve as a player. I pointed out in the message that Jesus Christ was beaten and bruised as He bore the punishment for our sins on the way to the cross. That is something I never could have done with my own dad. I knew better than to ask him because I knew that emotionally he could not handle that kind of aggressive interaction without it escalating into something far more than what it was intended to be. With Nathan, it was totally instructive. I had to motivate Nathan for the playoffs by telling him that everyone on the team had contributed to the success of the season and every player is needed for quality practices to take place. One parent remarked to me that his son told him that you had to practice hard or you would lose your starting position.

The players practiced that hard. He was right. It was an intensity that would last from Nathan's sophomore year through his senior year.

Our battalion is going to stop doing a lot of the Iraqi police training at the police stations. Some of our companies are being shifted to other missions so we are losing some of the companies under us, but not completely. We still have administrative control over them. They won't be responsible to us for what they are doing as far as their missions are concerned. I am hoping that as a battalion, since we are relatively small in numbers, with only 68 in our battalion headquarters that we could leave at any time. God is answering our prayers and over time, we will see it. Renay reminded us again that she is praying over the roster of the soldiers in our battalion and for the humvees that we ride in. Coach Niblett, too, says that he is praying for me.

The battalion we were to replace had been extended, but they are leaving soon now. Folks are being moved around a lot. One of the units under us is being moved to the Green Zone. Wouldn't it be great if our mission changed and we were sent home early? That might just be wishful thinking on my part. A general came by and said they are really changing things up around here. Not that we've done a bad job. It's just that the managers are going to change. "What's left for a Headquarters Detachment to do except to come home to their wives and children and eat hushpuppies and barbecue?" Renay asks me.

June 12

Found out yesterday that the First Cavalry is taking over all the MP work in Baghdad. Don't know yet what it means for us. Hope it means it will end soon. Talked to Renay for the first time using head phones over the Internet so now I can actually hear her talking.

June 13

Nathan and I got to talk about the spring game a little bit more. I told him I hope they can get a bigger lineman at nose tackle. Nathan said they were looking at someone that they thought might have speed. I still don't think Coach Niblett wanted to go all out for the spring game because he didn't run any special plays.

June 15

Nathan worked out this morning at school. He told me what his workout schedule was like.

June 16

I finally sense God's presence with me this afternoon and feel Him saying, "Just keep trusting." I sensed He was saying "keep praying" and I feel it really matters. Renay agrees. She tells me, "God speaks to us when we really need Him to. Things are bearable and just get better. I am so glad He spoke to you."

June 17

June 30th is just around the corner. Sensing a change in mission here, but not quite sure what it means. It is a time to be much in prayer during this transition that God would intervene in a mighty way. Mathews and I have spent 40 days in prayer leading up to the 30th. Mathews and I are brothers in Christ. He is what I refer to as my battle buddy. A battle buddy is a person that you pair up with when you have to walk outside at night. I am my brothers keeper and he is mine.

I sent Nathan an e-mail because he's on a mission trip:

Thanks for cutting the grass around the house this summer. I know you have been working out hard for football, but it will all pay off this fall. You will gain a lot from it in the future. I hope you have a great choir trip. It's good you can serve the Lord in this way. You are the best son a dad could ever have. If I have learned anything about being here in Iraq it is that we just can't pray enough.

For Christ in Baghdad,
Dad

Nathan wrote back and said:

Thank you so much for the letter. It was a great encouragement. I know you love me very much and I love you very much. Thank you for all you have taught me through the years. I know you are the best dad a son could ever have, and I thank God that He gave me you. I am working my hardest at football workouts, and I am cutting the grass every one to two weeks. I pray if it is the Lord's will you will be home by football season. I know that if it was not for you I would not be the person I am today. I love you very much and I want you home very, very soon.

Love your son,
Nathan

In Genesis 4:9, God reminds Cain of his brother Abel. We are our brothers keeper. Nathan and I are experiencing the brotherhood of the battle in a war zone and on a football field.

Spending time visiting with soldier

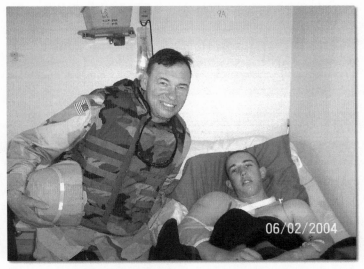

Praying with IED'd soldier at the CSH
(Combat Support Hospital) in Green Zone

Chapter Two
MY BROTHERS KEEPER

June 18

This afternoon I was thinking about going over to the finance office to get some spending money, but instead I decided I would check my e-mail. As I was sitting in front of the computer, I heard five loud BANGS. I knew there was some construction work going on upstairs and thought that was what I heard. Then I noticed a lot of scurrying about. It was then I knew it was actually a mortar attack. I quickly retrieved my body armor from the chapel and sat back down to wait it out. I didn't want to wonder too far.

The mortar shells landed right behind my building in the area of the 127th MP Company's maintenance shop—the direction I would have been headed in just moments earlier! Soon one of our senior NCO's (non-commissioned officer) hurriedly walked in and told me, "Chaplain Carroll you've got to go to the medical clinic. We've got a soldier down." I immediately started running toward the TMC (troop medical clinic), body armor and all, and met up with Major Compton. When I ran into the TMC, a nurse was waiting for me at the door to rush me into the ER. I walked in and found a young man lying on a stretcher with tubes in him. A nurse was giving CPR and a pool of blood lay beneath the stretcher. The chances of survival looked slim. All I could do was pray. It was hard for me to get up close to him with all the medical personnel that were working on him, but I was determined. I managed to take hold of his foot and prayed for him. I prayed hard that God would spare his life. At this moment I was thankful for an experience I had as a student at the Beeson Divinity School while doing CPE (clinical pastoral experience) at Baptist Montclair in Birmingham. I felt prepared.

I continued praying, thanking God for the people in the Friendship Baptist Association who were praying that God give me strength in a crisis like this. A moment later the doctors decided to fly him to the CSH. I told Major Compton that we needed to take a convoy to the Green Zone to be with him. When we got to the hospital, however, we were informed that he hadn't made it.

The soldier's name was Ty Vue and his memorial service was the first I would conduct while in Iraq. I had really prayed I wouldn't have to do one. While preparing for the service, I found out that Ty was from California. His dream was to go to college and then to law school. When he asked a friend what she would be doing a year from now, she said she planned to be married. He told her he planned to be on the beach soaking up the California sun. Ty would have been out of the Army before he went to Iraq, but, because of the Army's Stop Loss program, he had to stay on active duty. Spc. Harrison, my chaplain assistant, and Chief Jeff Mathews were my right-hand men in helping put this and later services together.

June 29

On Erin's birthday, I watched her open her birthday gifts via the web cam. She was on a choir tour last week, and we weren't able to get together to open her presents. We were in the middle of this online celebration when an explosion occurred. I hated this for Erin, but I had no choice. I had to put my body armor on. Rockets were being fired into our FOB (forward operating base). I found out from the other chaplains that there were two rockets. One had gone through the roof where a sergeant from the First Cavalry was working at his desk. Thank goodness, it didn't explode. The concussion only knocked him against the wall. He went over to it, kicked it, and said dispassionately, "Okay, let's get back to work."

July 1

The Fourth of July is just a few days away and the First Baptist Church of Oneonta wants me to call and say a few words to the congregation from here in Baghdad. Jack Green is getting the audio portion ready for me to make the phone call. I am going to speak a few short words about what I am doing here in Iraq and thank them for all the care packages they have sent.

July 9

There isn't much going on here right now which is good. One mortar attack last night. First in a while.

July 10

Some of the National Guard troops were really upset that they were extended. They even had to have a mental health team come in to talk to them. One of their soldiers was killed by an IED because he was riding in a soft-skinned, unarmored humvee. I thought those guys were going to have an all-out mutiny. But as soon as the ring leaders were discovered, they were separated and got more help. A soldier from another unit came to me about some of these same issues. He didn't want to be extended. I suggested that he talk to the mental health team. As it turned out, his unit didn't get extended and he went home as scheduled.

July 11

There are trouble spots all over Iraq at this time, mainly in Fallujah and with Sadar and Saddam loyalists. Even though Sadar has backed off, his militia is out of control. Renay says the support for the troops at home is at an all time high. I don't really see or know this except through the cards, care packages, and mail that I receive.

Renay's mother sent a number of prayer cards for me to hand out to all the soldiers in my unit. They really appreciate them, but I'm a little discouraged. Renay encourages me. "God is our only help. He is the only one that can tell us what He will do to help us." she tells me. "I know that you are seeking a word from Him and that is what keeps me going."

July 14

All the Iraqis are doing the police work now. We are speculating that we might get to come home in November. That would be great. I have received 23 boxes from the churches today to give out to the soldiers. The insurgents are attacking the Green Zone more because of the handover to the Iraqis.

July 15

I have moved from my old room into a room in the chapel. Chaplain Wilkerson has done an outstanding job. The chapel is going to be repainted and new tile will be on the floor. It's going to look great when it's finished.

Nathan did his physical for football today. They said he weighed 218 fully dressed. He probably weighs about 210, but he is where he needs to be now. Nathan's workouts included sprints of 100 yards and 200 yards. They are called "gashers". I don't know why. He was proud of his times. Linemen have to run 200 yards in 42 seconds and the 100-yard in 20 seconds. "Ratliff made his times and Will Posey was a little ahead of him from what I could tell," Nathan tells me. "Good," I tell him. "Ratliff needs to make them because the defense needs all the speed they can get." Nathan agreed.

July 18

Had a worship service tonight and read from Genesis Chapter 3. I told a creative story and then made spiritual application. It made for some interesting discussion. Sermons like that always remind me of my experiences in Baptist Campus Ministries when I was in college and of Bob Ford, our campus minister. He had a unique preaching style. Renay keeps reminding me that the people at home are really praying for me. "Everybody is focused on you and what you are doing," she tells me.

July 19

Chief Matthews is a good person to talk to when things get tough here. We have the same mindset, especially spiritually. Nathan is working out a lot for summer practice. I told him to be sure and tape his ankle for the upcoming lineman camp he is preparing to attend.

July 20

One of the saddest things that has happened is the ambush of two young girls that cleaned the main chapel. I had met them and talked to them just in passing. They were always around the chapel whenever I went to the post chapel meetings. They were very nice young people and would have been a joy to have in a church youth group. In a chaplains' meeting I was told that the car they had been riding in was stopped, they were drug out of the car, shot, and killed. This happens often to Iraqi workers on the base.

July 21

We have to wear our body armor whenever we walk outside of our barracks. Normally we would only wear it after nine o'clock at night. I attended a memorial service for a soldier from the First Cavalry who was killed when a rocket propelled grenade hit him in the back while on patrol. A young Hispanic man from Texas, he was the gunner in an uparmored vehicle. The body armor stopped the RPG from penetrating his body, but the impact caused the internal injuries that killed him.

July 22

Nathan went to lineman camp this morning. If they're going to win a state championship this year, the linemen will have to do it.

I remember Nathan's first year on varsity, his sophomore year, was notoriously difficult. This was the year Nathan went up against some super sized players that were on the team. These lineman outweighed Nathan by about fifty pounds and could easily push their weight around. There were times that Nathan put some punishing licks on those guys and it only made them angry. They would try to grab Nathan when a play was whistled dead and slam him to the ground. Whereas some players would stop their aggressive play because they did not want to be on the receiving end of their retribution, Nathan would not. Appeasement was not possible under the circumstances.

One day one of these Goliath's took a smaller player, turned him upside down, and somehow the student slipped from his grasp and fell to the ground smacking his face. The student received a black eye. Many a day Nathan did not even want to go to practice because he knew what he was going to face. Practice could be blistering. So as not to develop an aversion to practice, I told Nathan they were only making him better and to try to learn from them.

Being taunted by the older players and being roughed up as a scrub on the second team offense was not fun either. Eventually, Coach Niblett scrapped profanity from the team's vocabulary. I watched Nathan practice a lot. Nathan would say, "Dad, come watch me practice. Since I don't play in games, practice is my game." If I went to practice and saw Nathan standing on the sidelines not scrimmaging, I thought, "How's he going to get any better if he doesn't scrimmage?" Soon however, Coach Niblett would have him in the thick of things. Nathan's athleticism was confined to one sport, football. He exploited the opportunity to excel under the tutelage of Coach Niblett. Nathan was always about effort and effort was what Coach Niblett wanted.

I was a regular fixture when it came to practice. I was keenly aware of how Nathan was doing. Nathan's confidence often needed bolstering to sustain him for a long season of football. Every day before football practice that sophomore year, I offered support by praying and being mindful of what was going on at practice. Nathan saw little playing time that year. From a physical standpoint, the practice field was no sanctuary. The fact that he did not get to play much made it even more laborious. Nathan did not suit up to be a substitute. Nathan was not accustomed to being held in reserve.

Several of Oneonta's players enjoyed a lot of success during the year. Sophomore Miguel Hurtado, Oneonta's tailback, scored 28 touchdowns for the year and ran for a total of 2,050 yards. He accounted for 168 points scored. The year before, Miguel was a starting linebacker on defense. He caught everybody by surprise with his running ability. He would only get better over the next two years. Junior Drew Jackson, the quarterback threw for 1,327 yards and 13 touchdowns. Junior Zac Miller, a wide receiver had 39 catches for 582 yards and scored 9 touchdowns.[1]

---

[1] Chuck Gibbons, Football Sports Banquet Program, 2002

The defense was getting more ferocious with each passing game. Junior Stuart Sanders, a linebacker, started in every game that year after making some outstanding tackles behind the line of scrimmage during the Jamboree game, which was played prior to the start of the regular season. J.D. Whited was his usual self - going both ways at tackle on offense and defense. Zach Jones had a team high 47 tackles from his linebacker position. This is a team that was only going to get better in the days ahead. Nathan did get to play in several games when the first string got ahead in the game. Once when a starter was kicked out of the first game, Nathan was sent in to substitute for the rest of the game. That was really his crowning moment that year. He played about three quarters in that game and was in on a couple of touchdowns. His goal was to play in 16 quarters so that he could letter as a sophomore. He went in a few games, but never played as much as he did that first game. He went on to letter that year.

Would that life here was anything I was use to at home.

I had to move across the hall while the chapel is being renovated. The Iraqi workers are doing a good job. Unfortunately, my cell phone disappeared during this time. I know I sat it on the cot next to my bed so I could keep my eye on it. I hoped this would help me to keep up with it, but it disappeared anyway. The Iraqi workers had access to my room. I want to believe I lost it. When I tell Renay she asks, "Are people still treating each other with respect or are tempers flaring?" I tell her that Major Compton, who has a great attitude towards everything, is making things bearable. One day as we were walking to eat lunch at another camp, we met a group of soldiers. They saluted and we returned their salutes. There were so many I was doing it very fast, but Major Compton told me I was doing it too fast. Then she said, "You're doing fine." I could have taken it as criticism, but she wanted to be helpful without being critical.

July 23

Nathan went to lineman camp again this morning at Mountain Brook High School. It was like two-a-days. He compared himself to all the other guys that were there and felt pretty good about where he was. He said they hit dummies and held them for each other. Nathan held for a player that was 6'5" tall. When that lineman ran at the dummy, Nathan stood fast and didn't give him any ground. Nathan pushed back on the dummy to keep from falling down. Some of the guys that held the dummy for that same lineman were knocked to the ground, so Nathan felt proud that he was able to keep his ground.

There were over 200 linemen at the camp. Nathan said they do zone blocking differently. They step one foot back while we step one foot to the side, he told me. Renay felt really proud for Nathan and the rest of the linemen. Some of Nathan's teammates were unable to attend the camp, so she was proud that Nathan went.

Nathan said that the coaches did not call for prayer like Niblett does at the end of practice, so he rounded up his six guys for prayer. Renay could tell that camp gave Nathan a lot of confidence. He was able to practice on the very field where they were going to play the fall jamboree game with Dora. Nathan called Renay and was really upbeat. I felt they needed a camp like this because they looked so bad in the spring game.

Renay is hoping that Nathan stays healthy with his shoulder and ankle. She stressed to him about how important it is to stay healthy now. I remind her to caution him that the key is to keep his arm in so that it doesn't get knocked out of place.

Nathan would respond in an appropriate way once he knew what you were wanting him to do. Affirmation and a critique of practice were key to Nathan taking the initiative to become a better player. I would be truthful in sharing what was needed in the situation. Sometimes that was simply telling Nathan that he needed to get tougher on the practice field.

My own dad was another matter when it came to discipline. It was excessive, if not brutal. On one occasion, I took the lawn mower gas can to a neighbor because my friends and I wanted to put gas in a car and go cruising. Afterwards, I forgot to bring the can home and left it at my friend's house. My dad asked everybody in the family what had happened to the gas can. I told him that I had taken it to Robby's house to cut grass.

He could not control his anger and he kept asking me over and over, "Why did you do that? Why couldn't you just bring it home?" Then he said, "Get in the car, and let's go get it."

The closer we got to my friend's house, the angrier my dad became. My friend's house was just up the street and had it been any further the outcome would have been a lot worse. The more we talked about it the more it made him mad. I was sitting in the front seat of our white Ford Falcon station wagon as he drove. I remember that this car had a hole in the floorboard in the back seat of the car. He go so angry he finally hauled off and hit me in the eye with his fist. I went home and told my mother and she just said, "He shouldn't have done that." There was nothing she could do. She had seen so much of it she was almost numb to it by the time I was a teenager. Feeling the feeling of helplessness eventually emerged a strength on my part to defend myself and my mother against some of the more severe outrages.

There were times when he was too much for me to handle and I could not control him. Those were the times he would end up back at the Veteran's Hospital. I felt like I experienced life in reverse order; the preoccupation with what was going on at home was immense and distracting making it hard to stay focused and move ahead in life.

Childhood experiences had already shown me the damage of excessive discipline. When Erin and Nathan were growing up, I was always looking for better and more creative ways to correct them. With Erin and Nathan, it did not take much. They were the best of kids.

"I feel like everything is so messed up now," I tell Renay.

"Why do you feel that way?" she asked.

"I feel robbed."

"How?"

"Of time to experience things with Nathan during his senior year that I might not get to experience," I tell her.

"This is probably the hardest part for you," she says gently.

"It is," I reply.

Renay, ever the encourager, tells me: "This deployment is a big part of God's plan for your life. We have to believe that God is using His plan for your life in Nathan and Erin's life for their good as well, over time."

"It is very hard." I wanted her to know how much trouble I was having missing everything.

"But you are a tough guy and so is Nathan. God will use it in both your lives for His glory somehow for encouragement's sake."

I told her that I hoped Nathan would be able to turn it into motivation. Renay agrees. She thinks it could make him a tougher lineman as he looks forward hopefully to the November playoffs and the championship game when I may be home. Renay really believes I will be home then.

July 25

Talked to Nathan about his lineman camp. He spent some long hours out in the sun. They practiced for two hours in the morning and two hours at night. I told Nathan that he had to play a lot meaner than he did in the spring game. "Drive your man down the field," I tell him. "The more yardage Miguel gets, the greater your chances of winning the state championship." Nathan said it was like two-a-days. The other coaches had their own version of the same plays that Oneonta runs. They taught Nathan not to hop on pass protection, but to drive his feet like they do when they are run-blocking.

Renay tells me that Nathan has really worked hard and wants to talk to me about it but can't convey what he feels.

July 27

Nathan's football team is going back to the University of West Alabama for their football camp. He is glad that they will only have two in a room this year. "Praise the Lord," he exclaims. I asked Nathan who will be the backup quarterback this year and he said, "Probably Brent Bender." I asked him if he thought they would run more or be more balanced like last year. He said that Coach Niblett would always try to be balanced. I told Nathan that I think that keeps high school teams off-balance anyway. Most high school teams just like to run the ball. Nathan said that when it gets down to it, he will do whatever it takes to win, maybe with more running than passing.

"Y'all need to get better as the season goes on," I tell him.

Nathan responds, "I think we will—like last year."

I add, "I think the running game along with conditioning can win a lot of games." He agreed.

"The offense will have to win the first part of the season."

Nathan replies, "I think that is true."

"I think the defense will catch up," I answer back. Erin got in on the conversation and we talked a lot about her making CDs to send to me.

July 28

Renay asked me how Mathews is doing. I told her that he is fine, but doesn't like to sit with this one particular officer because as soon as he finishes breakfast, he blows his nose. Mathews happened to mention this to Maj. Compton one day and the next day or so we all happened to be eating breakfast with this one particular officer again. Sure enough, as soon as breakfast was over he blew his nose, and Maj. Compton promptly asked him, "Do you really have to do that?" Mathews would never say anything to the officer because he was too nice of a guy to do anything like that.

July 30

Seven mortars hit outside the base last night at 3:00 a.m. We returned fire. I'll preach this Sunday at the main chapel. About a hundred soldiers attend the services. I also conduct environmental briefings for soldiers who are taking a two-week leave.

August 2

Last night I was awakened at one o'clock in the morning by an officer knocking on my door. He told me that the commander wanted me to go with him to 31st CSH (a hospital in the Green Zone). Soldiers in the 127th MP Company had been shot. I didn't know any more than that.

I dressed as quickly as I could and grabbed the 40 pounds of body armor and my helmet. I didn't have time to get any water, which you really don't want to leave without. I wasted little time getting out to the truck. I inquired further as to any more details, but at that point there weren't any. I knew, too, that late at night was a bad time to be out on the road. The roads are the battleground. I got in a vehicle and said a prayer. We took off after a radio check and a stop at the gate for the others to load their weapons.

At CSH, the remaining details were filled in. Apparently, a squad from the 127th had gone out on a raid to arrest a suspect and confiscate weapons. As they were finishing up, one of the Iraqi policemen that was with them had not been exercising weapon discipline. He was swinging his weapon around when he accidentally pulled the trigger and fired three rounds.

There was a soldier standing next to IP (Iraqi policemen), and the bullets hit the marble floor they were standing on. When they hit the floor, they fragmented and went into both of his legs. Three other soldiers standing next to him were also hit in the legs. I was able to visit with all four, talk with them, and lead them in prayer. Afterwards, we took the four wounded soldiers back with us. I was so thankful to God that we could all go back together.

The next morning, I talked with my friend Peter an Iraqi man who comes to our building every day and owns a restaurant. Peter brings sandwiches from his restaurant and also sells Cokes and other items. The good thing about Peter is that he can speak English, which has made making friends with him fairly easy. He brings items we can purchase from him that we are unable to go into Baghdad and purchase on our own. Peter bought the linen cloth for our Lord's Supper table and a rug that I sent home to Renay.

During the time the last chaplain was here, a lot of people had been sending clothing and toys to distribute to the Iraqi people. These boxes of supplies had been stored in a closet that needed to be cleaned out. Nothing was to go to waste. I thought about Peter.

As I have come to know him, I have learned that he is a Christian and attends a Catholic church here in Baghdad. In some of the moments that we have discussed religion with a few of the interpreters, he has courageously declared to the Muslims, "Jesus is my God." When I thought about how I could get the boxes of clothes to the Iraqis, I thought about Peter. I knew he couldn't take everything at one time, so little by little, I had been giving him two boxes to take out through the front gate. Peter's pastor was making plans to distribute the clothes and school supplies and then take a picture of all the families receiving the clothes.

Our chapel has been repainted and new tile put on the floor. Peter told me that his pastor, Feris, wanted to donate pictures to our chapel to show his gratitude for the boxes. To show their appreciation, Peter had also brought a gift from his priest—a container that is used to burn incense. I was very impressed. I really wanted to meet Peter's pastor, but knew that it might be risky for an American to show up at his church and for him to be seen working with an American. It might be better for the priest to come here. Peter told me that last night a car bomb exploded in the parking lot of his church, killing his priest and several members of the congregaton. One of Peter's sons was wounded but he is doing fine.

We often get mortared on Fridays. When the insurgents go for worship they are insighted to attack. I've lost count of the number of times. One day the mortars landed on the back corner of our building where Peter sets up his shop, knocking out the glass in the building. No one was hurt though.

August 3

Worked on my Bible study for tomorrow and Nathan called Renay from his football camp at Livingston and gave me an update. Nick Ratliff is playing nose tackle. Nick has good size and can plug the hole up the middle of the defense. I asked Nathan about Nick Logan and he said he wasn't sure about him. Jake Jones is playing both ways. Nathan wanted Renay to tell me that Coach Niblett and one other coach said that he was doing a good job. I wanted to know when they said that and Renay said that it was after practice. I told Renay that Coach Niblett and the coaches are just going to have to encourage Nathan like that.

August 5

I was leaning against the wall of my building trying to make a call when I heard a buzz over my head. I knew what it was before my brain could translate the sound into danger and tell my feet to run for cover. When I was finally able to run, I heard the explosion somewhere behind me. CPT. Kasker, the commander of the 410th MP Company, was standing right behind me when we ran for cover inside our building. I was able to reach Renay and told her what had just happened. She asked me when it happened and I told her it was a second ago. She said she had been praying for me the past 30 minutes.

"I am so thankful God protected you, I have been reading Psalm 18. I've been up since 6:00 a.m. praying for you. How are you doing right now?" she asked. I told her I was doing fine and the insurgents were probably a mile away when they launched the rocket. Renay asked where Chief Mathews was and I told her I would probably see him in a few minutes and tell him.

Renay continued, "Yeah, guess what else happened last night. Nathan gave his seven-minute devotion. He kept stressing salvation. Coach spoke after Nathan and two were saved. Nathan said that when he started sharing his devotion, he could sense it was good."

I told Renay, "That's what needs to start happening." She agreed. Then she wanted to know how I was feeling. I told her it was nerve racking to hear that rocket go over. I had to go to staff meeting. Renay then shared, "You are in the palm of God's hand." I told her to keep praying. I told her to be sure to tell Nathan that T.R. Miller lost their quarterback and their starting tailback from last year.

August 9

A cousin of mine has written to say that another cousin named Wayne Wrenn had passed away. She wrote:

> Debbie called my Mom to tell her about Wayne. I called Debbie later that day and she gave me the details as to what happened to him. I feel so bad. I had no idea that he had health problems. I haven't talked to anyone from Birmingham in a long time. The last time I actually saw you was when your Grandmother Carroll passed away and you all came to White Bluff. Last year, Sheila Gayle sent me a picture of you and the family when you were getting ready to leave for Iraq. That was the last time I heard from her. I do hope that you are in a safe place. Mom, Stephanie (my daughter), and I will keep you in our thoughts and prayers...take care, respond when time allows, but know that just because we haven't seen you in a long time, doesn't mean we've forgotten about you. I sure hope you get to come home soon.

I e-mailed her back and told her, "Thanks for writing. We have been mortared the past three nights. It let up for awhile, but now they have started the attacks on our base again. Please continue to pray."

August 12

Wrote to a neighbor named Julie and said, "I am doing fine. Just wish I could see Nathan play through this season. I was talking to Nathan on a cell phone last night while standing outside on a balcony when a mortar hit and I had to get off fast. That's the way it goes around here...Keep praying, Ernie

August 15

Received a note from the Nibletts:

It's been a couple of months and it's hard to believe its football season. We are going to truly miss you in the stands and the before game victory lines and especially the smiling face and encouragement you always give during the season!!! Nathan was truly a blessing to Coach Niblett and the others at football camp last week. On Wednesday night they had a service and Coach Niblett spoke. Then Nathan and Nick Logan said a few words. Coach Niblett said Nathan began to speak about his spirit pack and he was looking at it and how it looks like a shield of faith and the armor of God. Coach Niblett was so blessed by Nathan's words. Coach Niblett did not realize that it looked like a shield when he designed it, but isn't that how God works!!!! So Coach Niblett said that maybe their motto this year should be about putting on the full armor of God. I thought you might enjoy that story. We love you and are going to continue to lift you and your family up in prayer!

Coach Niblett and Karon

August 19

I was able to take Environment Leave from Iraq for two weeks. I left Iraq on August 19. By this time, Nathan had gone to two-a-days at the University of West Alabama in Livingston. I had prayed that I would be home for good from Iraq to see Nathan load onto the bus with his teammates as they rolled out of the parking lot to go to two-a-days, but this wasn't meant to be. One of the reasons that I went home on leave at this time is that I wanted to see Nathan practice before the first game of the season. I saw him practice the whole week before that first game with Glencoe. I wanted to watch how he moved on the field and how aggressive he looked. I was pleased as I watched him practice during the week. The main thing that I saw was that he just needed to get more spring in his legs and to hustle a little more. Other than that, I thought he was looking good.

I was also aware that in some ways, the players needed to be more focused as a team. Most of my perspective came from what Nathan was sharing with me. I felt like he had a good read on the team. Part of that perspective had to do with the fact that some of the players seemed to have selfish ambitions in mind even though Coach Niblett is adamant against self indulgence. It was easier for Nathan to see it from his perspective as a player than for Coach Niblett to spot it as a coach. Nathan was at eye level with the team. I also felt that Coach Niblett is always looking for a new thought to help the team find momentum the same way a commander gives a briefing to his men before a military operation. I had given some thought that I would like to share a word with the team before their first game of the season.

I went to Coach Niblett after practice one day and told him I wanted to share a word with the team. He gave me that time on Thursday afternoon before they went out for practice. This is something I never would have thought of doing, except that I believed that some of the experiences I've had in Baghdad would prove insightful to Oneonta's quest for a state championship. I believe that whatever is going on in your life, that that is what you take to the field and play with. If you're into drugs and alcohol, you're going to take that to the field and play with it. Of course, you are going to lose if you do. Losing is what Oneonta did until Coach Niblett got control of the Oneonta football program. If you're a selfish individual, you're going to play a self-centered, self-serving style of football that is going to blame everyone else except yourself when things aren't going right.

What is going on off the field can have a huge impact on a team. What a lot of people wouldn't see and know is that Oneonta had a player whose dad was in Iraq serving as a chaplain and that was going to impact Nathan. How? Of course, that is a question that's going to have to be answered each and every week. It was going to make a huge impact on Nathan, this team, and Coach Niblett himself. That was a journey that we were all about to embark on and only God could answer that question. Only He knew the outcome at this point in time.

August 27

I went into the field house and all the players were dressed out in their blue and red walk-through uniforms. They were sitting around a locker room that is about as worn out as a field house can get. Surprisingly, the players' attitude toward such dilapidated facilities is positive. I had three pages of notes prepared, but never once looked at them. I hoped that I wouldn't have to because I knew if I did, I would lose some of the focus I wanted to maintain with the team.

I told them, "I believe that one of the first things I learned from all the games the team played in last year up through the state championship game is that every play is a potential touchdown. That's the way you need to approach this season. Right now, every game is a playoff game. Get out there and get the job done. How? The same way you survive on the battlefield in Baghdad is the same way you survive on the football field."

"First of all, you've got to be the biggest, baddest, meanest guy out there. Just as you have to constantly be paying attention while on the battlefield, you have to be on top of your game every minute and don't ever let your guard down. The terrorists are always looking for the easy targets to attack. They don't want a head-on confrontation. They want the easy prey. The philosophy of the terrorist is, "If you're hungry, why go after a lion when you can have a lamb?"

I said, "Pay attention, man your weapons. Know what each other is doing. Just as there are proper gun barrel clearing procedures to follow when you are loading or cleaning your weapons, that same weapon discipline carries over onto the football field as you execute a play. You are all depending on each other to maintain discipline as you carry out blocking schemes and run and pass patterns. Play hard but play under control. You be the dominant players on the field."

"I have been asked many times if this deployment changed me in any way. Not really. I experienced some things I've never experienced before. I'd rather think of myself as making an impact on others for the Lord's sake." I told the team, "Don't let these other teams come in here and make an impact on you. Rather, you make the impact on them. Never underestimate your enemy. As the enemy in Iraq changes his tactics, you have to be on guard to adapt to changing strategies by opposing teams. Be ready to adapt to these changing dynamics on your battlefield, the football field."

"Second, you are your brother's keeper. I do a lot of suicide prevention briefings for soldiers in Baghdad. Every soldier has to receive a suicide briefing within three months of being in theater. I'm not saying that anyone here is having a problem with contemplating suicide, but there is a parallel between certain suicide prevention techniques and preventing a team from self-destruction."

"I always talk about knowing the signs of suicidal behavior. This might be the loss of interest in hobbies, giving away prized possessions, and withdrawal. Some of the triggers of suicide are family problems, discipline problems in the unit, and being upset with loss of rank. How do you help prevent suicide? Know your battle buddy. It is the person that goes with you when you are out after dark. The battle buddy is a sidekick that watches your back. You need to be in pairs. Furthermore, if someone gets disciplined, you wouldn't want to isolate them and talk about them as to discourage them. Don't avoid that person. Don't ostracize him. Rather, encourage that person. Don't just say, 'Well, that's just their little red wagon.'" Help them. Encourage that person. Don't gloat in someone else's misfortune."

"This team could self-destruct emotionally and spiritually if the players on this team play for selfish reasons. Have a buddy system. Find a battle buddy and stick with him. Get to know him. Watch out for each other and care for one another."

"Third, give your best. Some of the soldiers in my battalion, like Ty Vue, lost their lives in combat and are not much older than the players on this team. Many of them are only a couple of years out of high school. Ty Vue was a young man from California that lost his life one Friday afternoon while working on a vehicle at a maintenance shop right behind the building where my chapel is located. Pray for Ty's family and friends as they deal with their loss."

I told the players, "If the soldiers can sacrifice their all, can you give your best for this team? If others can go to Iraq to fight for freedom to allow you to stay home and play football, can you not give of your best? Coach Niblett is trying to help this team. Allow him to tell you what needs to be done."

"I often had others tell me I needed to zip up my parka or sign out of the barracks or tell me something is wrong with my uniform. I could just as easily take this as criticism and have gotten very offended, but I realized that they were only trying to be helpful. That's what Coach Niblett is trying to do with this team. He is simply trying to steer you young men in the right direction, toward a relationship with God and a state championship."

When I finished my pep talk, Coach Niblett gathered the players around me. They all put a hand on me, and Coach Niblett led us in prayer.

That Friday night was the first game of the season for the Oneonta Redskins. The opponent that night was Glencoe. I got to the stadium an hour early. The hot dogs and hamburgers were on the grill. There are times that you might as well eat supper at the game because you want to savor every minute of the event—even the stadium food. That's what the avid Redskin fans do. Redskin fans get to the stadium early to give the opposing team something to think about as the opponent is warming up!

The football stadium, built in 1972, is carved right into a mountain. The stadium seats sit right on the slopes of the steep hillside into which the stadium seating is framed. When you sit on the home side of the stadium and look across to the visitors side of the field, you see one of the foothills of the Appalachian mountains into which the visitors' seating is built. There are small boulders that the children of the visitors are aptly warned over the loudspeaker to stay off.

Before the start of Nathan's junior year, the school decided to rework the stadium field. Seed was planted and dirt was hauled in to create a slope for better drainage. When the team got back from two-a-days at the University of West Alabama the field still wasn't ready. It's like you would go to practice just to see if the grass had grown any overnight. The field looked more like Daytona Beach than a football field. The first few games of the season had to be moved to the opponent's stadium because the condition of the field wasn't suitable for playing. Since frost doesn't hit until later in the fall, the grass continued to grow a few more weeks before any games could be played on it.

I was all over the stadium snapping pictures as Nathan stretched out. I took as many pictures as I could of practice and so that when I got back to Iraq I could put them on a bulletin board outside of the chapel for all to see. I did all the regular things, like stand in the parents of players' line as the team marched out from the field house to the playing field. Nathan was a team captain—a distinct honor for him and me.

The Redskins lined up to crash through the huge banner that cheerleaders painted for the team to run through onto the field and Oneonta's Redskin mascot was excited beyond himself. The entire student body, parents, and other fans emptied out the stadium seats to go to the field for the victory line for the players to run through. When the team ran out onto the field, they ran straight to the 50-yard line to lay claim to their field. They came to protect their honor and their dignity.

Glencoe kicked off to Oneonta, and three plays later, Anthony Mostella scored from the 45-yard line. This was the first touchdown of the season. Oneonta then kicked off to Glencoe and, after a defensive series, Glencoe punted to Oneonta. Oneonta stalled and Glencoe took over. The defense held. Oneonta drove down the field, the offense stalled and David Barnett kicked a field goal from the 7-yard line of Glencoe. The score was now 10 to 0 with 3:48 left in the first quarter.

Oneonta kicked off to Glencoe and forced them to punt from their own 45-yard line. Brent Bender blocked the punt. The following series Oneonta failed to convert on fourth down. When Glencoe got the ball, Oneonta's Adam Vincent intercepted the ball at the Glencoe 23-yard line. On the second play after the interception, with the ball inches from the goal line, Anthony Mostella scored with 9:49 left to play in the half.

Miguel Hurtado did not play the first half for disciplinary reasons. Chris Franklin played a lot at tailback and did a great job. I have always felt that

Chris plays well at a running back position. They need to throw more to him because he has great hands. On the junior varsity team, he never dropped a pass thrown to him. Sylvester, Miguel's younger brother, played well also.

At half time, the radio announcers were summarizing the game and noted that Miguel's first half suspension was over and he would be playing in the second half. Rob Rice said of Miguel's return, "That may liven things up a bit."[2] Mike Criswell made note of this [3]and said, "That offense may have stuttered a little bit in the first half and now that stutter may become a hum."[4]

In the second half, Glencoe completed a 55-yard pass and got the ball down to the Oneonta 6-yard line. On third and goal, the Glencoe quarterback dropped the ball and Oneonta recovered the fumble. Oneonta drove down the field, and Brody Cornelius scored from the 7-yard line with 4:33 left in the third quarter. Glencoe got the ball and was driving down field, but fumbled at the 41. Josh Gargus recovered the fumble at the Oneonta 41. That ended the scoring.

Nathan played his usual aggressive style of football. Oneonta won 24 to 0. It was good for the defense to get a shut out.

I spent every second I could at the practice field that next week before the Locust Fork game. Nathan had another good week of practice.

On Wednesday night, Nathan went to the Men of Will Bible Study at Coach Niblett's house. There the players always eat a snack supper which has increasingly gotten larger every year. Parents are sending more and more for the players to eat. Those young men respect and admire Coach Niblett and look forward to the fellowship with one another.

September 3

Game day came and the pep rally was conducted immediately prior to school letting out for the day. I gave Nathan my usual pep talk. We got to the stadium early and claimed our seats. It had been raining that afternoon and, as game time arrived, there was a heavy fog settling down on the field. I squeezed into a seat along the-50 yard line. The accommodations are not designed for the comfort of the fans of an opposing team. The way the home team looks at it, the fewer the fans the better.

I got a sneak peak at Nathan while he was having his ankle taped. The players were milling about outside the visitors' side of the locker room. I waited for Renay to walk into the stadium with Erin at any time. I chatted with

---

[2] Rice, Oneonta vs. Glencoe, WKLD, Oneonta, Aug. 27, 2004

[3] Oneonta vs. Glencoe, Video Tape, Alpine Advertising, Aug. 27, 2004

[4] Criswell, Oneonta vs. Glencoe, WKLD, Oneonta, Aug. 27, 2004

Nathan for a moment and then walked back to my seat. The raincoats and ponchos were everywhere as people were anxious for the rain to stop and for the game to get underway. I remembered when Nathan was a sophomore; it seems like it rained practically every Friday night. A wet, muddy field was always to Oneonta's advantage since they have a good running game.

Locust Fork kicked off to Oneonta and then Oneonta did what they do best...score. Miguel Hurtado scored on a running play from the Locust Fork 37-yard line. Oneonta stalled and with the ball on the Locust Fork 22, Oneonta tried a field goal and the kick failed. When Locust Fork turned the ball over on downs, Oneonta's Miguel scored from the Locust Fork 26-yard line. Oneonta kicked off and then got the ball after a Locust Fork punt. Sylvester Hurtado fumbled the ball and Locust Fork recovered at their own 43. Locust Fork fumbled on the very next play and Oneonta got the ball right back at the Locust Fork 47. Oneonta drove down the field and scored again in the second quarter. Oneonta kicked off. On the first play that Locust Fork ran, Oneonta's Brent Bender intercepted the ball at the Locust Fork 40-yard line. Miguel scored to complete the drive. Locust Fork had the ball after the kick-off and was forced to punt the ball again. Miguel scored again from the 7-yard line of Locust Fork. Oneonta now led 35 to 0 to end the first half.

In the second half, Brent Bender scored from the 13-yard line on a pass from Brody Cornelius. The starters are out of the game by now. This was the last time I would get to see Nathan play. The final score came from Sylvester Hurtado from the Locust Fork 39-yard line. The only score for Locust Fork came on a fumble recovery that was run back for a touchdown. Oneonta won 48 to 6.[5]

September 8

I returned to Iraq from after two-week leave. The two weeks I spent in Oneonta were the longest I had been home since January 2 of this year. While I wasn't able to get around to seeing everyone, I did see many folks around town as well as those at the football games. Things were very hectic when I returned to Baghdad. I had enlisted my Chaplain assistant and another soldier to conduct worship services for me in my absence. Chief Mathews filled in for me for the Wednesday night Bible study that night. I knew I wouldn't have time to prepare, not knowing for sure when I would get back.

I walked into the chapel and noticed Chief Mathews was in a conversation with someone. I greeted him and asked if he was ready for the Bible study. I had not even set my bags down when he informed me that there had been a

---

[5]This analysis based on review of Video Tape, Alpine Advertising.

casualty the day before.

One of our soldiers from the 127ᵗʰ MP Company had been out on a convoy when the patrol passed by a burning vehicle. The convoy commander decided to turn the convoy around to check it out. When they got to the site of the burning vehicle, now engulfed in flames, one of the other soldiers asked Lt. Price if he wanted her to check on the vehicle. He told her no that he would do it. A sniper fired two shots. One was intended for the gunner on top of the vehicle, but missed. The second shot rang out and Lt. Price was seen falling forward. The other soldiers thought that he was going for cover under their vehicle. By the time they got to him, he was dead. I will conduct my second memorial service.

September 10

Oneonta played Leeds High School at Oneonta today. Leeds, wearing white jerseys with green numerals and green pants, lined up to kick off to Oneonta. After three offensive plays Oneonta punted to Leeds. Leeds threw a pass from their own 23-yard line and Oneonta's Lucas Coffey intercepted the pass and ran it back for a touchdown with 9:44 left to play in the first quarter. Oneonta led 6 to 0. The extra point attempt failed. Oneonta held Leeds on the next series and forced them to punt the ball. On the next series, Brody Cornelius fumbled the ball and Leeds recovered. Leeds, on a fourth and one from the Oneonta 11-yard line, ran the ball and the running back was crushed by the Redskin defense led by Cameron LaRue. The score remained 6 to 0 at the end of the first quarter.

Anthony Mostella scored from the Leeds 20-yard line with 9:39 left to go in the second quarter, and after a failed two-point conversion Oneonta led 12 to 0. Oneonta kicked off to Leeds, and Jamal Lockhart ran the kickoff back a hundred yards for a touchdown at 9:21 to go in the second quarter. Oneonta had the ball after Leeds kicked off, and then Oneonta fumbled at their own twenty-yard line and Leeds recovered. On fourth and nine from the Redskin 27-yard line Nick Logan smashed the Leeds Quarterback back on the 34-yard line, and Oneonta took over. The offensive line began to open up some big holes, and Tommy Warhurst, the radio announcer, said, "What an excellent job by the line. There's the unit of Jones, Pierce, Carroll, Vincent, and Whited. What a great job they are doing."[6] Don Camp kept up the barrage of compliments by saying, "That Oneonta Redskin line is about to wear Leeds down."[7] A few plays later Anthony Mostella scored from the Leeds 2-yard line.

---

[6] Warhurst, Oneonta vs. Leeds, WLKD, Oneonta,, Sept. 10, 2004.
[7] Camp, Oneonta vs. Leeds, WLKD, Oneonta, Sept. 10, 2004.

The score was now 19 to 7 in Oneonta's favor with 2:05 left to go in the first half.

Oneonta kicked off to Leeds. On a third down play, Nick Ratliff ransacked the Leeds quarterback and forced Leeds to punt the ball away. Two plays later Brody Cornelius hit Lee Sims on a 31-yard TD pass. Oneonta was ahead 26 to 7 with fourteen seconds to go in the half.

Oneonta kicked off to Leeds to start the second half. Adam Vincent ended the series for Leeds after he dumped the Leeds quarterback for yet another loss. The inevitable happened for Leeds, and they had to punt. Oneonta ran off several more plays and reached the Leeds 5-yard line. Brody Cornelius threw a five-yard TD pass to Brent Bender, bringing the score to Oneonta 33 - Leeds 7.

After Oneonta kicked off to Leeds, and the Greenwave had the ball at their own 5-yard line. On the very next play Cameron Larue sacked the Leeds quarterback for a 2-point safety. Oneonta now led 35 to 7 with 6:34 left to go in the third quarter. Leeds had to kick to Oneonta. Anthony Mostella scored from Leeds' 13-yard line with 3:09 to go in the third quarter. Oneonta was ahead 41 to 7.

Oneonta kicked off to Leeds. Oneonta got a pass interference call and Leeds scored with 9:15 to go in the in the fourth. The game ended with a 41 to 14 victory for Oneonta.[8]

---

[8] This analysis based on review of the Video Tape, Alpine Advertising.

Ty Vue Memorial Service

Home for 2 week leave

Chapter Three
UNDER ATTACK –
GROUND ZERO & THE END ZONE

September 11

I flew my chaplain's flag on the roof of our headquarters building in honor of those fallen on this date in 2001. My unit and the whole FOB is on alert for an increase in attacks. Intelligence briefings have been warning to expect more enemy activity. On the morning of September 11, 2001, I was downstairs in the basement putting away painting supplies that I had used to paint the back porch of my log home. I was listening to the radio as I worked and didn't give it much thought that the DJ's talking point was New York City. Nothing seemed unusual at first, but then I noticed the discussion about New York was extensive. I noticed that I was not hearing the regular car commercials using an impersonator that sounded like former President Bill Clinton throwing the main punch lines, nor the phone pranks being carried out by the morning radio host.

The radio personality kept talking about the World Trade Center Towers and slowly it began to make sense to me that something had happened. It wasn't totally clear, but what I was hearing was that there had been a plane crash at the WTC and that one of the towers was down. I had been to the WTC when I was a summer missionary in 1976 and had visited it several times. I went back again when I completed my Chaplain Officer Basic Course at Fort Monmouth, New Jersey. That is when Renay flew up to meet me and we planned to drive our van back down to Alabama after I processed out the next day. Before we left for Alabama, I took Renay sightseeing in New York City to see the WTC.

I knew from having visited the WTC that there were radio towers on top of the buildings but had no comprehension as to the significance of what the radio host was talking about. I thought he meant that one of those radio towers had been hit by a small plane. When I went up stairs and turned on the TV it all became apparent as to what he was talking about. I could see then that one of the buildings had already collapsed and the other tower had been struck by a plane and black smoke was pouring out of it.

I was flooded with memories of that summer of '76 when our nation was celebrating its bicentennial celebration. I was serving as a summer missionary with several other college students from Alabama through our campus ministry program known as the Baptist Student Union. Renay was serving in Gadsden, Alabama, at the Etowah Baptist Association as a summer missionary working in the area of community ministries.

I spent most of the summer painting the New York Metropolitan Baptist Association office. We had a subway ride to the association office and back everyday from Brooklyn where we lived at the Park Slope Baptist Church. We were there for the whole summer to visit places like the Statue of Liberty and see the tall ships from the world over that sailed into the harbor there in New York. Some of the best memories of my college years were moments away from lying in ashes. I stood there watching this terrible scene unfold on TV. I walked back down to the basement and by the time I walked back upstairs the second tower had collapsed. The cause and the reason for all of this had not yet been revealed. Why, how, or who would be the question for sometime until it became apparent as to what had happened. It wasn't over yet. A short while from then we all would learn that there was a plane in the air over Pennsylvania that had terrorists on board with brave Americans willing to do what they could to stop the madness. Not only would this plane go down, but another would strike the Pentagon. All our lives were touched by the tragedy of that day. The question my family was asking is, "Daddy, are you going to be called up?" As a member of the Alabama Army National Guard I had to tell them that the possibility was very real that I might be called up since this act of terror was so horrendous and had affected so many people. I can remember after the Iraq invasion hearing the need for Chaplains to go. I wondered if I should volunteer. Many soldiers are dying in Iraq and here I sit at home. Little did I know that the orders to deploy were around the corner. My eagerness to deploy would meet with the harsh reality of the separation from loved ones, my son's senior year of football and the ministry I enjoy as a Director of Missions. Nathan and I are feeling the attack. I am experiencing the attack of ground zero and my son feels the fight to the end zone.

September 12

I asked Nathan if he is still excited about the win Friday night. Renay said they see the prize in front of them. I have tried to figure out how to listen to the game without it being on the Internet. Nathan has tried to put the web cam up to the TV so I can watch the game. It's too blurry. He has to describe the action to me through instant messages. This is the third game of the season and a good showing for Oneonta. Miguel did not score a touchdown, and I'm disappointed for him. I asked Nathan if Miguel was upset that he did not score. He said he did not know, but if I know Miguel he is a good sport and will do whatever it takes to win. I thought the offense did a good job, and I wanted to know if Leeds was surprised they lost and if Oneonta was surprised they won. Nathan just enjoys winning. Coach Niblett made the offensive line adjust to some new blocking schemes which had Nathan and the line confused. They seemed to adapt. The team always plays better than what Coach Niblett gives them credit. He is a perfectionist when it comes to football. Renay says,"Nathan knows Coach Niblett will yell at them at film study today so he is not excited about that, but they know they are getting better and plan to get to Birmingham." Nathan said, "Coach said if anybody thought they played their best, then we have problems." I told Nathan they still did well. "You had them 26 to 7 at the half, so that was good."

Renay and I are trying to come up with a way for me to see the games since it takes the mail about two weeks to reach me. The only way I can know anything about the games live is if I get up in the middle of the night and call Renay several times.

I told Erin that I have a memorial service for Lt. Price on Monday. Then Renay got back online and said, "I know that will be hard, but God is helping you do His will there." I told her it's just hard to be here. I'm still tired from jet lag."

Renay asked, "Have you had any rocket attacks since you have been back?"

"Every day. The insurgents are having a field day."

Renay then said, "That's sad. I guess that's why I woke up several times last night and prayed for you until I fell back to sleep."

We have to wear our body armor outside now all the time. I asked Renay if Deborah, my younger sister, got to stay after the game to see Nathan. She said that they left in the third quarter. They usually don't get to stay for the whole game. Deborah is a nurse and is on call a lot.

I wondered if Nathan is excited about the season. Renay commented, "Nathan is not really excited because Coach Niblett blessed them out Friday night. He did not really celebrate the win with them. Coach Niblett usually doesn't if the win isn't perfect." Renay went on to say that, "Coach Niblett criticized them a lot because I think he was disappointed that the linemen did not execute the blocking schemes he taught them. He may be frustrated with everything. Nathan is not really excited right now. I keep telling Nathan that it was good, and he got five pancakes. Those are a big deal to Nathan."

"But you know he is glad?" I ask.

Renay replies, "Oh yeah! Nathan knows what a win means. The pancakes help him feel better about his part. Nathan is pancaking the size players that end up getting scholarships."

Renay then started talking about the hurricane that is going to affect their weather on Friday. The weather forecasters are predicting that it will move from the Gulf straight through Alabama.

I can't stand the bombs.

September 13

First Lt. Timothy Price was killed on September 7, 2004. This was his second tour of duty in Baghdad. He was an outstanding soldier. I conducted his memorial service today. What does a chaplain say that can bring comfort to fellow soldiers at a time like this? I recall the words written by the publisher in the foreword of Don Nori's book, *The Hope of a Nation That Prays*, reflecting on September 11, 2001 he writes, "We will get through this, we will do more than survive. We will grow through this. This whole experience will cause us to grow in our respect and love for one another and toward God. We will emerge many times the leaders we were before this atrocity. We have the will and we have the faith. We will resolve to be more committed to family and nation and we will come together in a way that makes us a more formidable foe."[9] God will help us get through these trials.

The memory that helps sustain us when we reflect on patriots like Lt. Timothy Price, reminds us that he was a person of conviction who had pride in what he did. The life he lived is a labor of love for and a devotion to his fellow soldiers. Lt. Price was a citizen, and because of his personal convictions, became a patriot. Lt. Price's patriotism did not rest on his opinion but on the principle of participation.

What makes him and all soldiers courageous is that he reported for duty. It was his duty to serve his country in Iraq, and he answered that roll call. When the time came for campaign rallies back home in America, Lt. Price was not a part of the crowd that was waving the flag in unison with sound bites, but was carrying the flag that he wore on his right sleeve into battle. His patriotism did not begin and end at the ballot box. Lt. Price died for the American flag.

---

[9] Nori Don, Treasure House Books, (Shippensburg, PA: Treasure House, 2001),5

The Word of God sustains us during times of grief for our fellow soldiers. The resurrection of Christ is the hope that we offer to others in times of grief.

> And if Christ has not been raised, our preaching is useless, and so is our faith. More than that, we are then found to be false witnesses about God, for we have testified about God that he raised Christ from the dead. But he did not raise him if in fact the dead are not raised. For if the dead are not raised, then Christ has not been raised either. And if Christ has not been raised then your faith is futile, you are still in your sins. Then those who have fallen asleep in Christ are lost. If only for this life we have hope in Christ, we are to be pitied more than all men. But Christ has indeed been raised from the dead the first fruits of those who have fallen asleep." (1 Corinthians 15:14-20, NIV)

Nathan said that he saw a picture on the web of my unit getting our combat patches. I was on leave at that time and missed the ceremony. I wanted to know how practice went, and Nathan told me that they went till about 6:15 p.m. Nathan thought they had a good practice today. At the end, they went one-on-one—something they had not done since two-a-days. I wondered why they had gone so long, and Nathan told me it was because they have to get better in the coach's eyes. Nathan said that he hit his defensive man and drove him back three or four yards, and he didn't get to the ball carrier. Nathan said he had to go a lot against the better linemen on the team. They never got to Brody on their pass plays. I said, "Those linemen are good ones to judge how you're doing. If you block them, you can block anybody. If you go up against the best on the team, it will keep you sharp."

Nathan said, "That's why I say I had one of the best practices because I went against the starting defense."

I told Nathan that I sent the Iraqi Freedom t-shirts, plus one for Coach Niblett. Renay told me that he would like that and that he prays for me every day.

I told Nathan to tell the offense to score on every play. Every play is a touchdown. I mentioned to Nathan that the playoffs are played differently than the regular season because every play is played like it's overtime. Play as though each play could be the deciding factor between moving to the next round or hanging it up for the season. Play like you intend to score.

Renay thinks the team is doing a great job and not to worry. Then she said, "Coach told me that Nathan had a really good practice." I really want to get the stats on the metro teams in the Birmingham area. Renay is putting them into the mail to me. She wanted to know if I wanted her to call Ron Ingram at the *Birmingham News* and ask if they can be found on the Internet. I told her to try doing that.

I asked Renay if anyone had asked about me at the game, and she said, "Ernie, God is in control of this. He knows what He is doing with our lives. He is not confused or delayed in what He is doing. We have to trust Him. It really hurts badly for you and us, I know, but it is our faith and not how bad it hurts that will pull us through this." She went on to say that Mike Cornelius prayed for me at the Quarterback Club meeting tonight. I told her in the worst of situations you have Jesus to walk with you like in Psalm 23, "through the valley of the shadow of death." Not death but the valley of the shadow.

I said, "There are no answers to the prayers, only help in enduring the trial." Renay said that Nathan really enjoyed talking to me. "He knows you would be here if you could," she said. I told her to tell Nathan that blocking people on the Oneonta defensive line is a key to him staying sharp. They are that good.

September 14

We are in our body armor all the time now. The insurgents are firing on us through holes cut in the roofs of their houses so they won't be as easily detected. Just hate it for Nathan that I can't be there for his season. Renay said, "Nathan will be okay. God would not permit Nathan's dad not to be here if God could not handle it in Nathan's life."

September 15

Nathan had a great day at practice. I wanted to know how it was good. Nathan said he did good in team period and inside, and then good on third down situations against the ones. I asked him if he had any pancakes and he said he had three. Coach Niblett got mad at the line. "Coach told me good job after my third pancake." I told Nathan there were situations where he needed to drive his feet faster, as fast as a lawnmower blade moves. For instance, the man he is blocking is more likely to go down if he's driving his feet faster. As the game goes on, I told him to drive his feet harder with each successive play and as he gets closer to the end zone. Don't stop driving your feet until the whistle stops blowing. The other player is going to pause at some point in the play and when he does that's when he's going to be able to finish off the block by knocking the defensive tackle backwards.

Nathan said, "A day of three pancakes is pretty good."

I respond, "Sounds good, just keep your head up. Remember to hustle. It's important to establish a good pattern before the fourth and fifth games. Nathan agreed. I thank him for the Redskin report.

September 19

This is the week of the Susan Moore game, the biggest rivalry in Blount County. Nathan has film study at 2:00 p.m. He may go out in pads today because Coach Niblett lost a couple of practices due to bad weather. I told him this is a big game. Nathan filled me in on some of the college action going on. He said that Alabama's Brodie Croyle is out for the season. Auburn beat LSU 10 to 9.

I work on my sermons, finish a memorial service, and feel under the weather. My throat has been hurting, and Renay encouraged me to go to bed. She said, "I'll just pray that God will send His blessings to you in your sleep like the scripture says."

September 21

Nathan had a good practice again yesterday, but right tackle Joe Willie Whited's shoulder popped out. I hated to hear that. Nathan said they iced it after practice. He thinks he will be okay. His parents will have to find him a shoulder brace like Nathan wears. Renay heard from Joe Willie's mother. He tore a ligament in his shoulder, but it has popped back into place. Renay was able to tell Joe Willie's mother about Nathan's experience with shoulder problems and what we had to do about it. She wanted to know if Nathan had to go to American Orthopedic where they make orthopedic braces. Renay said that Nathan went there to get fitted. Nathan also wears a shoulder pad to help with impacts. I told Renay to tell him to "keep his arm in and don't throw it out real wide. Don't just fling his arms out wild."

I asked Renay if Joe Willie's mom was glad to hear from her, and she said, "She really did. I was surprised she called me back so quickly. I told her I would bring Nathan's brace for her to take a look at so she could see what she needed. She sounded like she was just trying to get him ready for practice today."

I heard the Oneonta Guard is being deployed to Afghanistan. I was part of this unit before being transferred to the 231st MP Battalion. I am going to try to call Nathan on the phone about his practice. I would like to help him process each practice as he goes through it. The practices are as big as the games when you want to win the state championship.

Renay tells me, "That is so true and Nathan works so hard at them. They practiced for three hours yesterday. Nathan just wants to tell you how he did in each practice."

I tell her, "You can't imagine how much I miss not being there to experience this with him."

"I know this is the hardest time for you and Nathan," Renay replies.

"Anything I can do to be a part of this would be a big help."

"Talking to him each night would help him process his day," says Renay.

September 22

I asked Nathan about practice and he said it was pretty good and a little better than the day before. He did about as well as he could, but I tell him that doesn't sound very motivating. Nathan said, "I had one play where I didn't understand that Matthew Pierce was pulling to the left, and I didn't block the nose man. Coach stopped and asked what happened and he told me what to do." I asked Nathan if he thought he did better, and he said he thought so. I told him just to stay focused on what he was doing.

Nathan said, "I'm just praying that I'm ready for the game, which I think I am." I remind him that not staying focused is what gets people killed here (in Iraq). Then I ask about Joe Willie, and he said that he was back at practice today. He is wearing a vest like Nathan wears. Adam Vincent was practicing, too. I tell Nathan to drive his feet and stay focused. Nathan tells me he tried to drive his feet until he heard the whistle on every play. The Susan Moore football team said that they will beat Oneonta this week by two touchdowns, and that Miguel's number is going to be 12 instead of 21 when they get through with him.

I got my combat patch today. Of all the rewards I have received, the combat patch is the most meaningful. I am now a combat veteran.

September 23

This is a message I sent to Nathan on the eve of Oneonta's game with Susan Moore.

To Nathan:

You're the best, number 66. We have spent a lot of time talking about football, watching film, and praying through all the ups and downs, but God has blessed us. God has given you a great opportunity to play for such a wonderful

Christian man like Coach Niblett. You have worked so hard and accomplished so much, and the best is yet to come. Please know that all the prayer warriors here in Baghdad are praying for you.

Remember, every play is a touchdown!

"BE STRONG IN THE LORD AND IN HIS MIGHTY POWER"
(Ephesians 6:10, NIV)

September 24

This is going to be the first time I will get to hear Nathan's game on the radio. Renay had to put a microphone up to the radio, so I could hear it over the Internet (I had to do this until the Oneonta radio station's website was working). It sounded like I was at home listening to an Alabama game over the radio. It's going to be party time in Baghdad tonight because I can hear tonight's game against Susan Moore. Renay told the radio station that I could hear WKLD's radio broadcast, and told them to say hello to me in Baghdad. I could hear Danny and Terry giving the news. They said they would tell Rob Rice and Mike Criswell to tell everybody that I was listening in from Baghdad. This is huge for me. God does answer prayers. Renay is concerned. She tells me, "I'm afraid everyone knows what our family is doing now. I'm going to keep the security system on all day and night. Everybody knows you're in Baghdad, and we are all at the pep rallies and ball games." My sister Deborah and her husband Ronnie can't come to the game tonight, but Renay's mother is there.

Mrs. Horsley said that she wrote Nathan a note that said if Mr. Horsley were alive today he would be at every game. Renay tells me that she thinks her mother is grieving some for me in Iraq and for Renay's dad, so she's coming to the game. I got the seniors on the team some T-shirts from our base, and Renay hopes that Coach Niblett will give them to the seniors today instead of waiting until Sunday.

As I'm listening, the game is about to get underway and the radio announcers are commenting on the fact that the kids from both sides are lined up in their respective victory lines. The fans seem to be having a hard time keeping lines intact because the students are mingling with their friends from the other school. The momentum for the game is building. Mike Criswell announces, "That motivation ends after that first hard lick. Yeah, you lose all that excitement when you're looking out the ear hole of your helmet."[10] This was going to be a tough one for Oneonta.

Oneonta kicked off. Susan Moore punted after their first series. Then Susan Moore held Oneonta and forced them to punt which Susan Moore blocked. Oneonta held on fourth down after Susan Moore failed to convert at the Oneonta 24-yard line when a pass attempt fell incomplete. Oneonta got the ball back, moved the ball to the Susan Moore 6-yard line, and attempted a 24-yard field goal that was no good. Oneonta finally got on the board with 11:13 to play in the first half. Jorge Marquez kicked the field goal.

On the next series Nick Ratliff and Jake Jones had some key quarterback sacks forcing Susan Moore to punt again. When they did, Oneonta's Adam Vincent recovered a fumbled punt return. Oneonta got the ball at the Susan Moore 33-yard line. Oneonta moved the ball to the Susan Moore 29-yard line. On fourth down, Brody Cornelius threw a TD strike to Lee Sims. OHS then kicked off to Susan Moore, and on third and nine, Oneonta's Lee Sims intercepted the ball at Oneonta's own 18 yard line. Susan Moore came right back and intercepted a pass. A few plays later Lee Sims intercepted again for Oneonta at the end of the first half.

Susan Moore kicked off to start the second half. The score in the second half was when Anthony Mostella scored around the left end with 5:58 left to go in the game. Oneonta beat Susan Moore 16 to 0. Brent Bender had to go in for an injured Brody Cornelius to play quarterback.[11]

September 25

Nathan is thankful that they beat Susan Moore, but he has some mixed feelings about his contribution. He had some good plays and some bad plays, but overall I think he knows he did well. Susan Moore really got after Oneonta. They wanted revenge for last year's loss. Nathan said they would put out six or seven men up on the line of scrimmage and send a linebacker in as well. Number 58 got to the ball carrier about four or five times. I asked Nathan if he was making sure he was driving his feet and he said he did. Number 58 would line up between Nathan and Matthew Pierce, and Nathan would have to just try and cut him down as he worked down the line of scrimmage. Renay said Nathan blocked number 58, but nobody picked up number 88.

I told Nathan that all they seemed to want to do is take away the line of scrimmage and force Oneonta to go wide. That is what Oneonta was doing, and they had a lot of success going off tackle. They just wanted to

---

[10]Criswell, Oneonta vs. Susan Moore, WKLD, Oneonta, Sept. 24, 2004
[11]This analysis based on review of the Video Tape, Alpine Advertising.

take away the inside. Nathan said that he never allowed his man to get to the quarterback. "We should have just kept running to the sideline." Nathan went on to describe how aggressive Susan Moore played and that they had either six or seven men in the box at a time. The one thing Oneonta learned from this game is how to deal with so many men on the line of scrimmage. They got better for it. Because Oneonta played in a state championship game last year they are big targets for opposing teams this year. Josh Niblett would say, "You've got a big target on your chest this year, and that's the way it's supposed to be."

I'm buying all the seniors on the team T-shirts from here in Iraq. We both agreed that I would get them for all the seniors. Nathan wants to wait to give out what he has already received in the mail for when Coach Niblett cools down and is not so upset with the offense.

I had to leave the base today because one of our soldiers died of natural causes. He is in one of our companies over by BIAP(Baghdad International Airport), and I will have to conduct his memorial service. My sermon needs a lot of help. Renay said, "I will pray now for your sermon like we prayed for Nathan's football." I told Renay to tell Nathan that Coach Niblett will try to rotate him with other players during scrimmage just to make him mad and get him fired up.

September 26

Had to go to Camp Victory tonight for an anniversary dinner of the MP Corps. It was in one of those big palaces that Saddam Hussein built. Since it is Sunday night, my Chaplain Assistant, Kenneth Harrison, filled in for me. I rode back to our FOB with Capt. Kasker from the 410th MP Company out of Ft. Hood, Texas. A lot of military vehicles get IED'd at night. When we got back to the FOB, Cpt. Kasker asked me how I had liked the trip. Without giving me a chance to answer he said, "That's good stuff." The danger gives him an adrenaline rush.

I preached this morning at the main chapel and really felt the presence of the Lord. I could see people were listening attentively. During the Lord's Supper I was holding the trays and just felt the Spirit come over me. Several people came up to me and said they thought I really did well. Major Compton came up to me and said, "Boy, you did a good job."

There was a reporter from Massachusetts in our worship service this morning. I thought I noticed someone walking around taking pictures. After the service, when most of the people had gone, one of the chaplains told me that this reporter is an atheist and was shot at last night. The round entered the vehicle because the driver had the window open. This reporter said that

God spoke to him during the service.

Renay said that she got up at the same time that I was getting dressed today to specifically pray for me. She set her alarm at 1:00 a.m. to pray for the service at 10:00 a.m. (Iraq time). Then Renay told me that she prayed that God would anoint me for the day. I feel like people that were in the service this morning said that God had spoken to them as well. God just touched the service this morning.

I told Nathan that I thought the football game Friday night was the best thing that could have happened to Oneonta. It shows how people are gunning for Oneonta. It should motivate the team and the coaches to get better.

September 27

Renay said that Nathan is doing fine. He's putting a lot of pressure on himself. Coach Niblett has put in a lot of new plays for the upcoming Springville game. Nathan doesn't have a good handle on the new plays. I told Nathan he needs to work hard driving the bigger players on the team off the line of scrimmage to compensate for people on the line. I still think Susan Moore played the line of scrimmage. Nathan needs to give himself more time to pick up on those plays. I think the new plays will keep the opposing teams off balance. Nathan said, "They stopped the run and forced Brody to throw and every time we were out numbered on the line. They blitzed their linebackers too."

I tell Renay that I think Nathan just needs to keep playing smash-mouth football. She thinks Nathan did a good job. He may have missed a few blocks, but everyone else did too. He didn't get any penalties. "It went so fast you couldn't even follow the play," Renay noted. I remind her that they just need to slay the giants before them.

Renay went to the Quarterback Club where Coach Niblett tells them that it's not the *county* championship that they're after; it's the *state* championship they want. Most teams are only after a county championship anyway. Coach Niblett said they would be ready for the Springville game. He went on to say that Oneonta needed to set a tradition of being regional champs. Renay said that Coach was upbeat tonight. Brody Cornelius won't play quarterback Friday night—Brent Bender will. Coach said that with Springville they cannot wait to score as they did with Susan Moore or they will be out of the game in no time. Springville will score fast and a lot. I'm hoping that Nick Ratliff can stay in the backfield of Springville.

Everyone at the Quarterback Club was shocked that I heard the game over the radio. Renay said, "I saw a great play that Nathan had when I looked on the tape. It was when Bender had to go in for Brody. Nathan blocked a guy really well that was going at Bender, and Bender got away. But then another guy got him."

I tell her again, "They just need to slay the giants before them."

Renay said, "Right and prayer is the real answer. We need more people praying. Now we are getting injuries, and I'm not sure we see the real need here."

September 29

Injures are hitting the Redskins. Miguel was limping during Friday's game against Susan Moore, and now it looks like Brent Bender will have to go in for Brody Cornelius at quarterback. Nathan got out of practice 30 minutes early today because the first string had to go the whole way and so they were sluggish at practice. Coach Niblett feels like they need to rest.

October 1

Today was the game against Springville. It was a hard fought game. Springville kicked off to Oneonta, and the game went back and forth. Oneonta had the ball at their own 39-yard line when Brent Bender handed off to Anthony Mostella who ran the ball 59 yards to the Springville 9-yard line. Five plays later Anthony Mostella scored on a fourth down play from the 3-yard line of Springville with twenty seconds to go in the first quarter. The extra point failed, and the score was Oneonta 6, Springville 0. Oneonta kicked off to Springville, and Springville's quarterback scored from Oneonta's 27-yard line on a quarterback option play. Springville missed the extra point tying the game. After the kick off to Oneonta, play resumed at Oneonta's 24-yard line. Because of some excellent blocking on the part of the offensive line, key runs were made. Brent Bender made one on a quarterback keeper from the OHS 45 to Springville's 23-yard line. Oneonta was forced to settle for a field goal with 21 seconds to go in the half. OHS led 9 to 6.

Oneonta kicked off to Springville for the opening of the second half. Springville and Oneonta each had turnovers for the opening series of the second half. Oneonta had good field position with the ball at the Springville 40-yard line. More blocks by the offensive line moved the ball to the Springville 16-yard line. They held, and Oneonta was forced to go for a field goal. They missed with 3:22 left to play in the third quarter. Two plays after Oneonta gave the ball over to Springville, Oneonta's Adam Vincent intercepted a pass. He fumbled it on the return trying to swap hands. Oneonta stopped Springville on a good defensive series when Springville had the ball on fourth and seven at the Oneonta 18-yard line. OHS got the ball back, but was stopped and forced to punt. Oneonta's Chris Franklin got the ball back when Springville muffed the punt return. The only scoring in regulation play came after Oneonta was called for pass interference and Springville's drive was kept alive. They were able to kick a field goal, tie the score, and send the game into overtime. OHS scored a TD in overtime, but Springville answered that score with one of their own. On the next series, Springville got the ball back and threw an interception to Lucas Coffey. Oneonta then kicked a field goal and won the game 19 to 16.[12]

October 2

I really feel left out of all the football stuff that is going on back home. Just not being there is hard. Renay said that the parents and fans all see me as almost being there as they learn that I am hearing it on the radio and when I can call in live on the score board after the game.

"You are a big part of this football team; the players all feel your presence and the men all hug Nathan and talk to him about you," she tells me.

"It is just hard for me not to be there."

Renay also tells me that this team is different than last year's team. Last year it was all about how they played good football. The senior moms prayed for the season all the way through. Now the boys are praying their way through. They see what Nathan has to do in leading spiritually without me there. This is helping me to feel better. The cheerleaders have put up a sign at our house that says, "Lead 'Em Straight, Nate!"

"Nathan is becoming a spiritual leader. Part of the reason is because of what he has to go through here without you." They say, "If Nathan can keep the faith then I can too." This year it is all about spiritual preparation and leadership. Renay asked if I can see how God is choosing to do this.

It is just hard to be here. Renay reminds me of Christ's words, "For then we have the strength of God in us, and nothing is impossible with God in us." It is hard to imagine how anyone can be in Iraq and not see the need for Christ in their life. An active duty captain who is a West Point graduate and our praise service leader, told me yesterday how much he appreciated my sermon on Sunday. That was a real encouragement for me. Renay said that it is what God used to show people that He is here with me. Renay says that if God is here blessing what I am doing like that, then He must know how we both feel right now. His presence is here to bless what I was saying, and that

---

[12] This analysis based on review of the Video Tape, Alpine Advertising.

it is a powerful thing. God is reading each word we write and He knows the plans He has to bring us back together again. We can't look at circumstances; we have to look to God.

Renay was encouraged by Coach Niblett's faith this week in spiritually preparing the team for the game against Springville. Renay said, "I truly believe if Coach Niblett hadn't, they would have lost the game." This year it is all about God, and God is trying to help us parents understand that. Renay thinks the boys get it.

I wanted to know if the people from Oneonta were excited about the games. Renay said that they were panicked at the end when it went into overtime. They kept asking, "What are we going to do? What are we going to do?" Renay told them to pray. She told them to pray above their ability because then they will know that God did it and not themselves. That's what God wanted last night. A lady who heard Renay say "pray" turned around to a mother who was cursing and told her to pray. Coach Niblett had prayed and had a real peace about the game. Nathan said, "This is the first time an Oneonta team has gone 5 and 0 since the 1980s. Coach Niblett has 41 wins and only 14 losses. He needs only ten more for the championship. Nathan said in the locker room when they broke it down, he yelled out, "This was a God thing!" Coach Niblett responded, "It sure was." Half the boys, especially the younger players, were saying, "God did this. Praise the Lord!" Nathan said that for the last two years it has never been like this, especially among the players themselves. Nathan, when the defense was on the field with 42 seconds to go in the game, knelt on the sidelines and started praying. Then Matthew Pierce knelt beside him and then another. Not all in the same huddle. But when they saw Nathan start to pray, they knelt where they were where and started praying, too. God is doing a great work on the team.

Nathan told Renay that he goes through a Springville game every day of his life without me there and that he kept encouraging the boys on the sidelines to "keep the faith." Nathan said, "We did not know how the game would turn out, just like we don't know when Daddy will be home, but I just keep telling them to 'keep the faith' and God worked it out."

Renay said, "Nathan knows God will work it out for you to be with us if we keep the faith, just like God did with this game. From the beginning of the season, Nathan has been pointing out the 'shield of faith' that is on their spirit pack shirts."

Nathan needs to realize that his practices are at a higher level than most other schools, especially at this point in the season. Renay tells me that Coach Niblett made the adjustments from last week's game; not just any coach could do that, especially without the starting quarterback. I think the team is reaching for a higher competitive level. Renay said it really was on a higher plane. Coach Niblett stepped up, and God told him what to do. God helped them to play their very best, beyond their abilities at times. I think they have more tools available to them than they realize.

As I was listening to the game over the Web, I heard a certain play that went to the left. The radio announcer said the line really blocked well and called Nathan and Jake Jones by name. Jake hurt his ankle. They put him on crutches, and Nathan said he was waving to them from the sidelines, cheering the team on. Nathan thinks he will be okay.

The 278th Chemical Battalion in Oneonta that I was a member of has now been activated and is going to Afghanistan to provide security there. They will find out deployment is nothing like a weekend drill.

October 3

During the Susan Moore game, Nathan had a lot of problems with their players submarining the line of scrimmage. I checked this out and shared some advice with him from some of the guys in the unit. I told him to cut down the angle of attack. Aim for the right shoulder as he is looking at his opponent. Get into the gap first. I asked Nathan if he did this, and he said that he fired off straight at him and then cut down the point of attack. He is always trying to get into the gap before the other player does, but he had to leap at him like a frog to get up under him and drive him.

If the player is trying to shoot the gap, then drive him down the line of scrimmage. I told Nathan, "If you sense the player is trying to submarine the gap between you and the center, then you have to drive him into the ground and down the line of scrimmage to the right. If that's where he's going, then use his momentum against him." I looked on the Internet for ways to help him. I saw articles about "ISO blocking." That's a term I heard Nathan use many times in referring to particular plays that they were using. I also heard him use "zone blocking." Football and its terminology has changed a lot since I played left tackle for two years at Woodlawn High School in Birmingham.

Woodlawn was about 15 miles from where I lived. It sat on the edge of a fast-changing neighborhood that now looks very much like the inner city. After my sophomore year, I transferred to Huffman High School, but I never played football there even though I thought about it. With a little more parental support and encouragement, I probably would have played.

On a number of occasions after practice at Woodlawn, I wouldn't have bus fare home so I would hitchhike back to Huffman. Sometimes I would bum a ride from my coach after a game. I never really knew where he lived; I just knew he went by my house on his way home.

My own dad never watched me play football. He could not relate to athletics because he didn't have the presence of mind to do so. Most things I had an interest in were out of his realm of experience. Having only an eight-grade education, he was more familiar with a sawmill than he was a school. As a disabled veteran of the Korean War, he slept most of the day because of the medication he took. When he wasn't sleeping, he would sit on the front porch, smoke, and drink coffee. He was on valium until the VA decided it was detrimental and took him off it. When they did, he went through withdrawal.

My dad was not a life coach. He did not have insight to share to help guide me in any decisions I made, nor to help me think about the consequences of those decisions. He couldn't give me advice on how to start a career or make career decisions. He never punched a clock, had to make staff meetings, go to trade shows or conventions, or worry about promotions. The one thing he did was to absorb what so many Americans didn't—the ravages of war. He died of emphysema (smoking helped calm his nerves). When the VA reassessed my mother's pension, she received a letter stating that even though my dad's death was not the direct result of combat; he did have a long-term disability, and she was awarded a benefit as though he had died in combat.

My line coach those two years at Woodlawn was a man named Red Little. I remember he had dark red hair and chewed tobacco all the time. He taught us two ways of blocking: scramble blocking and regular pass blocking. To avoid a penalty for holding, you had to hold your jersey when pass blocking. But now a player can use his hands more in pass blocking. At times it looks like he is taking a quick punch with an open hand at his opponent.

The pass stance and the pass blocking stances have changed tremendously. Instead of getting down in a four-point stance, the way we did in my high school days, players now get in a squat position with their hands on their knees and can use their hands more. That is fine to a point. A good body slam will work wonders against a defensive lineman.

Nathan was having a problem his sophomore year with some of the senior players on the team. They were using their weight to their advantage against Nathan. Rather than going head up on them, Nathan was using his hands too much to his own disadvantage. I told Nathan to quit being so handsy and get more physical. He might use his hands at first contact, but then when the defensive player came in the second time, he would have to use his body against the opponent to block.

If he had a blitzing linebacker, he would have to step up into him rather than sitting back and letting the linebacker get a running start toward him. An offensive tackle needs to do this to establish his authority on the line of scrimmage. He couldn't take his normal two steps or three steps back. He would have to adjust his attack by stepping up to meet the linebacker and lessen the blow from the blitzing linebacker that was coming at him like a raging bull.

The varsity was going over some offensive plays one afternoon when I saw a linebacker coming at Nathan pretty hard. I saw Nathan dip his head low instead of keeping his head up. It has always been our number one rule—keep your head up. After practice I asked Nathan about that particular play, and he told me he was trying to cut the defensive tackle. That's when I told him he needs to be more physical than handsy. Using a pass pro may be good on some instances, but he would have to get more physical and stick his nose in the player right at the line of scrimmage.

Football is a lot like a game of pool. Pool is not all about banking shots or trick shots. It's a lot like a chess game or playing checkers. If your opponent is getting the best of you then try to add one something to your tool box to play with; go for the easy shot instead of just blocking pockets on the table.

No matter what the sport, there is always some technique or strategy to incorporate into your game. In the last track meet that Erin my daughter competed in, I couldn't help noticing that one of the other runners running in the two-mile run ran right on the inside lane with her left foot almost always stepping on the inside lane stripe instead of the middle of the lane. This saved the runner a lot of steps over the course of a two-mile run. That girl earned college scholarships. She had a good strategy.

Our commander's personal security detachment

Hanging out with soldiers from the
410th MP Company, after a Memorial Service

Having fun with 89th MP headquarters at
Camp Victory before returning to Camp Falcon

Chapter Four
IN GOD'S HANDS NOW

October 7

The media is reporting an explosion outside the Sheridan in the Green Zone. The terrorists hit the targets that will give them the most publicity. It seems like the insurgents are trying to take over Baghdad the way they did Fallujah. The terrorists want to do as much damage as they can before the election in the U.S. Three times a week we have a BUB (Battle Field Update Brief). Not every enemy activity is reported. The SIGACTS (significant acts) can be anything from small arms fire, IEDs, RPGs, or grenade attacks. They happen all the time. Renay is praying that this will all be over soon. She prays that God will answer our prayers. She said, "God is our only hope. Somewhere along the line God will take all of this and tell us what it means. He has a reason." At times it seems it's up to God anyway, and anything we feel is irrelevant.

Renay said, "As a Christian, I know He does care. We aren't sure what the reason is-you, me, Erin, or Nathan, but I am trying to find out by praying it out...the meaning is something in God's will for our lives." Nothing happens to us as Christians by chance. Feelings don't help the situation, only faith does. We don't deny the feelings because even when we are applying our faith the feelings are still very strong. Don't deny them, but don't entertain them because that won't help. Do entertain and cultivate the faith.

"Ernie," Renay said, "remember when we were at Gordo church, and you were at the altar, and God said to you, 'I know how you feel, I was beaten too.' God does know how you feel and He just wants you to keep coming to Him and asking what He wants to say to you about this whole experience. The way home is through Iraq, and it is a straight shot home."

Renay continued, "God only knows how tough it is for you. But I believe if you and I will walk it by faith, you will walk your way straight home from Iraq."

October 8

The Pennington game was today. Oneonta seemed a little flat against Pennington in spite of what the score indicated. Pennington kicked to Oneonta, and on the first play Oneonta's Brody Cornelius ran a 72-yard keeper in for a score. The touchdown came with 11:39 to play in the first quarter. The next TD for Oneonta came with 6:44 to play in the first quarter on a Cornelius to Lucas Coffey touchdown pass. That made it 14 to 0 for Oneonta. Pennington showed some spunk running the ball in the second quarter. Pennington got on the board with a touchdown run from the Redskin 11-yard line. The Oneonta offensive line opened up some huge holes, and the running backs made big plays and got the ball down to the 1-yard line. The radio commentator, Rob Rice announced, "Oneonta's offensive line grew up last week against Springville."[13] That was true. When the ball was on the 1-yard line, Rob Rice said, "If Oneonta's center sneezes, the ball is in the end zone."[14] On the very next play, Anthony Mostella scored and Oneonta was up 21 to 7 with 8:22 left in the third period. The next touchdown came on an Anthony Mostella run from the Pennington 3-yard line. The score was now 28 to 7 Oneonta with 1:16 to play in the third quarter. The next TD was on a Miguel Hurtado run from the Pennington 9-yard line with 7:26 to go in the third. The score was now 35 to 7. An interception by Josh Gargus set up the next TD, which came with Brent Bender in at quarterback who handed off to Anthony Mostella, who ran the ball in from the Pennington 28-yard line. The score stood with Oneonta convincingly ahead at 42 to 7 and 4:49 to go in the third. Lee Sims intercepted a pass at the Pennington 26-yard line and ran the ball in for a defensive touchdown. With 1:16 to go in the third, the score was now 49 to 7. Finally, with 5:36 to go and all the second stringers in the game, Chris Franklin scored on a run from the Pennington 14-yard line. The final score was 56 to 7.[15]

October 9

Oneonta just played Pennington and won. Renay thought Nathan wasn't playing up to his potential, so she met him going into the field house. It wasn't that he was playing bad it's just that he wasn't playing as sharply as he did the week before. As Renay and Nathan talked about it, Nathan told Renay that he had dedicated the game to me. For some reason focusing on me became a hindrance. Renay told Nathan that he simply needed to play for himself and for God and to quit focusing on me. She reminded him that when I am speeding down the roads of Baghdad in the middle of the night going to the hospital, I am not thinking of doing that for them. Rather, I am focused on staying alive and doing what God has called me to do—my job. Nathan has to stay focused on staying alive on the field and doing what God wants him

---

[13] Rice, Oneonta vs. Pennington, WKLD, Oneonta, Oct. 8, 2004.
[14] Rice, Oneonta vs. Pennington, WKLD, Oneonta, Oct. 8, 2004.
[15] This analysis based on review of the Video Tape, Alpine Advertising.

to do for this team. It's not that we don't love and support each other, just that in the heat of the battle you have to remain focused on staying alive and doing your job safely and to the best of your ability. Football is the same way. He has to do it for himself.

I believe the win is for me, playing the game is for Nathan. How he plays determines whether he wins or loses. Nathan really needs to focus on how he plays the game-we will celebrate both victories: my coming home and his state championship, when I get home. Renay said the boys are more of a team and focused on God. Like Coach Niblett said, "God has His hand on this team."

Renay continued, "The morning you left in March from Fort Benning, the first thing that came to my mind was, 'we are in God's hands now.' I pray those two hands will come together and let you see these games." She tells me that we can't live by our feelings; only our faith will get us through this. "Feelings have to flow like a river—not get stuck or dammed up. To get across the river we have to have a bridge or something, and that bridge has to be faith." she reminds me.

October 10

We are not getting any mail because some of the mail escorts have been killed. They have to change the routes, so the contractors won't get the mail.

October 11

Had a rocket attack this morning and another tonight. I heard the one that hit this morning and I knew we had been hit again when they were getting accountability. This morning's was too loud to be a mortar. They said on the news that they were putting off some big operations until after the elections, so this is what we get.

Conducted a memorial service for Clifford L. Moxley, Jr., a 51-year-old soldier that died in his sleep of natural causes. He was from New Castle, Pennsylvania, and was assigned to Company C, 2/103rd Armor. Right before we got to Camp Victory to conduct the service, there was a rocket attack and a soldier in the 89th MP Brigade was killed.

October 12

I just received the Susan Moore game on tape. I thought Nathan did a good job. It all boils down to desire. Nathan just needs to keep doing the basics over and over. Nathan needs to realize that it's as if they are playing at the small college level. The crowds are more into the game, and the opponents are really having to play above themselves to try to beat Oneonta. Nathan needs to try to get better each week. He'll have to get better to win the state championship. I can't emphasize to Nathan enough about driving his feet.

Coach Niblett was mad because someone cursed while the team was at a recreation league football game. There was a team meeting before discipline work so that whoever said it might confess, but no one ever did. Nathan told the other players that they can't build a team if they can't trust each other. I was glad that Nathan spoke up because he is a senior and needs to be a leader.

Nathan had a better practice today and tried to keep his feet better and stay locked onto his opponent. He has to drive his feet and keep the opponent in front or to the side of him when moving down the line of scrimmage. The Susan Moore linemen tried to cause a stalemate and make the tackle. I told Nathan not to hesitate when he hits the defensive player, to hit him hard and as fast as lightning.

While I was upstairs on the balcony talking on the phone with Nathan, we were attacked. I told Nathan to hold on a minute and ran back inside my building during the mortaring. He asked me if everything was okay. I told him they will give the all clear in a minute. The subject turned quickly from the dangerous environment back to the one thing that takes my mind off the reality around me—football. I told Nathan to stay on his block and drive his man back. Do the basic things well and he will get that championship.

October 15

This is the day of the Sumiton Christian game and another win for Oneonta. The real story is that Oneonta's defense accounted for seven interceptions. Corey Richards had two, while Brent Bender, Josh Gargus, Lucas Coffey, Justin Bryant, and Colby Tipton each had one. Oneonta won 48 to 27. Miguel Hurtado ran the ball back deep into Sumiton Christian territory only to have the ball intercepted at the Sumiton 5-yard line. Oneonta got the ball back and moved it down to the 11-yard line. It was obvious that Sumiton Christian wanted to bunch up the middle, so Oneonta took advantage of this plan when Brody Cornelius threw a touchdown pass to Brent Bender from Sumiton's 12-yard line with 6:15 to play in the first quarter. Sumiton Christian came right back and scored a touchdown tying the game at seven all with 2:52 to play in the first quarter. The next score for Oneonta came with 9:21 to go in the half when Miguel Hurtado scored on a run from the 2-yard line, bringing the score to 14 to 7. The next touchdown was set up by a Corey Richards interception at the Sumiton 33-yard line with 6:14 to play in the half. On the next play, CJ Hubarer caught a TD pass, putting Oneonta ahead 21 to 7. The next TD was set up by a Brent Bender interception at Oneonta's 44-yard line. From Sumiton's 12-yard line, Brody Cornelius threw a 12-yard TD strike to Lee Sims. The score was 28 to 7 with 2:52 left to play in the half. Sumiton Christian came back with a touchdown of their own, ending the half at 28 to 13.

In the second half, an interception was made by Josh Gargus and the Redskins got the ball back at the OHS 38-yard line. Three plays later, Miguel scored from the OHS 48-yard line. The score was 34 to 13 after the missed extra point. Sumiton Christian then had the ball back on the OHS 38-yard line and Corey Richards made an interception, running the ball out of bounds at the Sumiton 2-yard line. Anthony Mostella ran the ball in from the 1-yard line upping the score to 41 to 13. Lucas Coffey made the next interception allowing Miguel to score from Sumiton's 2-yard line. Justin Bryant and Colby Tipton each made interceptions. Sumiton Christian went on to score two more times to make the final score Oneonta 48, Sumiton Christian 27.[16]

October 21

A lot of talk about the upcoming elections at home. Renay asked if I remember the Bible story about how Moses would raise his arm in prayer, and the Israelites would win the battle. But when he dropped his arms, they would start to lose. I said, "Yes, I know that story. It's in Exodus 17:8-16." Renay went on to say, "What I am saying is that you and I are getting weary, lifting our hands through this, and we are going to have to have people 'prop us up' in prayer to get to the end of this. I think that is where we are. We are near the end, but our arms are tired and nothing is helping us keep them raised. Family and friends are going to have to prop us up in prayer." Finally Renay said, "I'll prop your arms up if you will mine. We'll make it through this battle."

October 22

This is the day of the Oneonta–Ashville game. Renay and I are talking about trying to find a radio station that is broadcasting the game. Apparently no one is. Renay asks if we have had any rocket attacks, and I tell her no. Renay tells me she'll try the Leeds station again.

"There it went," I said.

"There *what* went?" Renay asked, concern evident in her voice.

---

[16] This analysis based on review of the Video Tape, Alpine Advertising.

"Rocket attack," I said. "It may have been a mortar."

"Why do you think *that*?"

"I wish they would stop this stuff."

Renay exclaimed, "God is protecting you! Right now He is protecting you! Right now He is doing that. Every moment you are there."

The guys in the 410th TOC told me it was a mortar. I had to call and report in. Renay tells me, "You are in God's hands—we are all in the center of His will, and that is the safest place to be." Renay was glad that I was not outside during the attack. She told me that Nathan had received the pictures of one of his games that I ordered off the internet and sent him. A lot of work goes into Nathan playing football, and Renay tries to keep Nathan going by attending every meeting, practice, and game.

Sharing it with me is the best part of it for them. Nathan handed out more of the Iraqi T-shirts I sent to the seniors and Coach Niblett. The players were very appreciative. I just hope and pray that Nathan gets to play in all 15 games that can be played. Just to be able to play in every single game will be rewarding for Nathan, especially since I can't be there. Just to say the team stretched it out as long as they could would be great. I hope that Winfield and Rogers get beat early in the playoffs because I know they are fired up from last year.

Oneonta beat Ashville 31 to 6. The biggest play of the game came when Oneonta's Nick Ratliff, a short, stocky player, intercepted an Ashville pass at their 16-yard line made it all the way to the 3-yard line before he was tackled. It was a huge interception and could have been bigger had Nick scored. But Oneonta fumbled the ball right back to Ashville on the very next play.[17]

It's hard to be here and not be able to go through this season with Nathan. It's even harder to serve in a place where people are trying to kill the members of your congregation.

October 23

The main chapel was hit by a rocket last night at ten o'clock. There were three chaplains across the hall from where it hit in the brigade chaplain's office. Chaplain Godwin-Stremler was watching TV across the hall and the rocket blew a huge hole right in the wall of the chapel. Had he been in his office, the rocket would have blown his legs off. Thank God, no one was injured. After this attack, huge concrete barriers were put up all around the main chapel.

---

[17]This analysis based on review of the Video Tape, Alpine Advertising.

There is a lot of talk about when the 69th MP Brigade is leaving. The U.S. is sending more troops from South Korea to Iraq. The British are moving some troops from southern Iraq closer to Baghdad. Who knows when we will finally leave? It's up to God anyway. I have been waiting for man to reveal it, but I know it will be more of a revelation from God when it finally does happen.

By beating Ashville, Oneonta clinched the region championship. Renay talked to Gail Cornelius about parents doing more to support the team. The kids respond more when they see the parents involved. They are going to take food to the film study tomorrow. I think the offense's experience is beginning to show. They are doing a great job.

October 24

I wish I had the Sumiton and Ashville tapes here. Renay asked me what the soldiers say about the war, and I told her they pretty much stay quiet. They are young and just want to do their job. Those who seem to have an opinion are in my unit. They have something to say about everything. The chapel that was hit by a rocket was a hard building. If it wasn't, the rocket would have killed everyone in it. "Except God did not let that happen," Renay said.

The crowd at worship was better tonight. I wasn't really even prepared beforehand, but I preached better than I was prepared to preach. I preached about Naaman the leper from Syria in Second Kings. The story said a good deal about pride. Renay said that she, Erin, and Nathan were praying for me the entire time. God is here, but sometimes I can't sense what He is doing to end this. Renay said that God is enabling me to do what I do here and God is enabling the Redskins to do what they do.

October 25

While I was on the Internet with Nathan, we had a mortar attack. I had to tell him to hold on.

Renay asked me, "Incoming what?"

"It's bombs as always," I tell her. "This is really getting on my nerves."

Sgt. Kendall came over to see if my radio was on for accountability. I told him it wasn't. I could tell he was irritated. He wants me to keep the radio on, so he doesn't have to walk over here to get accountability. It is dangerous to walk out during an attack. Now that we are getting bombed more often I am just going to have to keep it on most of the time which means I'll have to change the batteries every day. Because the radios aren't secure, we can't give names and exact locations during accountability. We are almost certain the enemy is listening.

I get back on the internet with Nathan and tell him that I think Oneonta will probably play Dadeville in the first round in the playoffs. He thinks so, too. Nathan practiced from 8:30 a.m. until 11:00 a.m. because there was no school. He said his practice was between okay and good. They have put in some new plays for Moody. I wondered what kind of plays and Nathan tells me like going around a combo block and going after the linebacker. Nathan said they were putting Nick Ratliff at nose along with another player to get Nick fired up. But Nathan never lets Nick get to the quarterback. "Nick bull rushes," he tells me. Cody Payne was put at nose tackle to give the scout team defense a look more like that of Moody because they have a really big nose tackle. Nathan said, "It was hard. I kept him covered up and got some movement out of him. I just have to get better." Cody plays long snapper on the team. Scott and D.F. Payne, Cody's dad and grandfather are the biggest Redskin Fans. I tell Nathan to look for Moody to be more physical than anyone else they have played. I cannot stress enough that if the ball is run up the middle, Oneonta can beat anyone.

It's difficult here to be around others that use foul language all the time. It's different from where I work back home. Nathan said that it's like that sometimes on the team, especially with the younger kids. They often use profanity. I told Renay to tell Nathan that he has to keep leading. Renay said, "That is what I told him. I told him that when Coach gives him a chance to speak, or he is talking about this team to the other guys, he needs to tell them that stuff like that is 'loser talk' and they will not win that way." Major Compton is home on leave. It will be better when she gets back. She and Mathews are the ones that make it bearable.

Pepsi is going to honor Nathan with a trophy this week at the pep rally. They had to put it off because of the hurricane a few weeks back. I asked Renay why they are honoring Nathan. She tells me it's because of what I'm doing and how Nathan is having to play without me. I'm glad that someone is going to do something for him in that regard. Renay said that she was glad that he gets something for going through this football season without his dad. I have pictures of Nathan on the bulletin board out in the hall. The people that live in the building with me are from Rhode Island. They are very complimentary of Nathan. They think he is a big guy. They've kept up with the Redskins the whole season by virtue of that bulletin board. However, an officer told me one day that he thought that I ought to take the pictures down because the bulletin board was a chapel bulletin board and not a personal one. I told him the only way that I would do that is if the commander or Major Compton told me to. Besides, it was a way for me to show soldiers that I was a family man and my family was very important to me. It gave us all, soldiers and myself, something else to think about. This was the only negative comment I ever had. I think the officer really felt bad about ever saying anything about it to begin with.

I have finally seen the tape from the game on October 8, when Renay met Nathan at the fence at half time to tell him to get his head in the game and quit thinking about me. Nathan wanted to know what I thought about him. "Nathan, you did a good job in the first half, but you did a *great* job in the second half."

Nathan said, "So, you think I did good?"

"If you block like you did in the second half, you will be a state champ."

Nathan, "Really?"

"You outdid yourself in the second half."

Nathan said, "Right, okay."

"Don't sell yourself short," I tell him.

I tell Nathan he needs to try to pancake on every play. I could tell that the more Oneonta ran the ball, the more rhythm the offense established. Nathan needs to move guys like he did in the second half and put them down field. What I saw in the second half is the Nathan I want to see more of. The second half is the key to winning the state championship. From now on he can't just block, he has to drive his man down the field. Nathan is good at doing that.

October 26

One of the Iraqi interpreters was caught spying today. A patrol came across a place where they had been firing mortars. They caught four of them. The Iraqi National Guard beat the captives until one of them started talking. They had been coming from Fallujah on these bombing missions every week. The insurgents said that one of the interpreters down the hall called him and told him two Bradley tanks were coming out of the base. The insurgents were waiting on the side of the road for the tanks to roll out when they were somehow caught. I saw a soldier sitting in a chair all day where they keep the bottled water. I finally asked him if he was guarding the water, but he said he was guarding an interpreter. The news has been reporting that the Iraqis are losing confidence in their government. The Iraqi people won't let their children come up to American soldiers because they believe they are targets of the insurgents and are afraid their children will be killed. Renay said that lots of people are praying for all the troops and that we are not forgotten.

October 28

The power has been off today. Something is wrong with the generators. It is so inconvenient when this happens. The power lines in the ground have been shorting out. Tried to call Adam Vincent, number 56 a linebacker on defense and a guard on offense for Oneonta, but no one answered. He had surgery on his foot and I need to have prayer with him. He is out for the Moody game which will be a physical game. Every team Oneonta plays from now on will be spitting fire.

They found out the water has E-coli in it and have made us stop taking showers. Sometimes the water lines up north get blown up and we can't take a shower until the water lines are repaired. I enjoy jogging and many days I have to wear my body armor while I jog, but it's still enjoyable. Chief Mathews jogged in the mornings until the summer, but the mortar attacks have become so frequent he had to stop.

October 29

The radio station is trying to set up the Moody game on the Internet. Being able to listen live is a tremendous morale booster. Nathan is excited about the game, but he always gets nervous. With Fultondales forfeit last week, Nathan is ready to play. Ronnie, my brother-in-law, is going to the game tonight. He is a tremendous support to Nathan. Nathan appreciates it when Ronnie talks to him at the fence around the third quarter.

Three plays after Moody kicked off to Oneonta, Oneonta scored on a pass play from Brody Cornelius to Lee Sims, shocking the Moody team and surprising the Oneonta fans. An excited Rick Sanders, who was calling the game on the radio, said of the TD, "I've got chills on my back."[18] Moody and OHS swapped series until Moody drove the ball down to the OHS 16-yard line. On one particular play during the series Sanders noted, "The ball carrier for Moody went down not wanting to take the punishment."[19] On the fourth down from the Oneonta 1-yard line, the OHS defense stopped Moody cold and took control back. On the very next play Miguel Hurtado ran for a 10-yard gain to the OHS 25-yard line. Rick Sanders said of the bruising running style of Miguel, "When you go to tackle Miguel, you'd better bring the student

[18]Sanders, Oneonta vs. Moody, WKLD, Oneonta, Oct. 29, 2004
[19]Sanders, Oneonta vs. Moody, WKLD, Oneonta, Oct. 29, 2004
[20]Sanders, Oneonta vs. Moody, WKLD, Oneonta, Oct. 29, 2004

body with you because he is a load to bring down."[20] Oneonta continued to move the ball behind some punishing blocks of the offensive line. Rick Sanders commented saying, "The offensive line is giving a strong initial surge knocking the Moody defensive line off the ball and allowing the OHS ball carrier to fall forward for more yardage. That's how dedicated the offensive line is."[21] OHS drove the ball down to the Moody 5-yard line where Brody handed off to Miguel for a touchdown. Rick Sanders, overcome with excitement, said, "Man alive! This is 14 to 0 with 6:37 left in the second quarter."[22] After OHS and Moody swapped the ball around, Moody scored with fifty-one seconds to go in the half.

In the second half after OHS kicked off to Moody, OHS forced Moody to punt. Oneonta got the ball at their own 44-yard line and drove it down the field to the Moody 1-yard line. Unable to get a touchdown, they attempted a field goal but missed. Moody was forced to punt after a few attempts at moving the ball. OHS got the ball at their own 47-yard line, and two plays later, were on the Moody 15-yard line. Rick Sanders, overwhelmed by the offensive line's blocks, said, "They have found a little seam in there that seems a little promising. Kinda of like when you're mining for coal. You find a seam, and you stay with it till it runs out. I'd stay with it right here."[23] On the next play, Brody Cornelius handed off to Anthony Mostella and ran to the Moody 5-yard line. Don Camp said, "Did you see Miguel Hurtado get that lead block on that play for Anthony and then Anthony pat him on the helmet? That's why this team is a championship caliber team. Those backs are fine. A lot of teams complain about carries. They don't care. Rick, they want to help each other block. I loved what I saw right there. This team, under the direction of Coach Niblett, has been molded to trust each other as brothers."[24] On the next play OHS scored on a 3-yard run by Miguel Hurtado with 32 seconds to go in the third quarter. The score was now 21 to 6 in Oneonta's favor. Moody scored with ten minutes left to go in the fourth quarter, making the OHS win, 21 to 12. The OHS defense had an excellent game, and Cameron LaRue continued to be a defensive standout by causing the Moody QB to fumble the football back to Oneonta. The Redskin's offense ate time off the clock, and the

---

[21]Sanders, Oneonta vs. Moody, WKLD, Oneonta, Oct. 29, 2004
[22]Sanders, Oneonta vs. Moody, WKLD, Oneonta, Oct. 29, 2004
[23]Sanders, Oneonta vs. Moody, WKLD, Oneonta, Oct. 29, 2004
[24]Camp, Oneonta vs. Moody, WKLD, Oct. 29, 2004
[25]This analysis based on review of the Video Tape, Alpine Advertising.

defense secured the win.[25]

October 30

Heard from my friend Ray Shackleford. It was really good to hear from him. He served in the military in Korea when he was single. Not with a family like I have now. Ray said that the closest thing to violence that he experienced was bar brawls by the soldiers themselves. However, there is one wartime experience that we do share—every day is one day closer to coming home. Called Renay and encouraged her. I scanned more pictures of Nathan playing football. People are nice enough to say something about them to me. That really helps.

October 31

Renay sent me some football stats. From my perspective, it appears that if Oneonta runs the ball, they could go all the way to state. We talked about the worship service for tonight. Then Renay prayed for me:

> Lord, we need You to help us. We need You to guide and direct Ernie right now and understand the direction You are leading him in this hour. We need to know, Lord, what this week has in store for any of these soldiers who come to You for a word. Lord, You know, and it is extremely important that You lead Ernie now to know and to do Your will. Some soldier may want to pray a sinner's prayer tonight in the quietness of his own heart. Something needs to happen here both spiritually and politically. Lord, speak to Ernie and me on having enough faith and belief in You to just get us through the end of this day. We don't have the faith to get through the whole month. Just for tonight's service. Amen.

Renay wanted to know if anything else happened today. I told her I went to a memorial service for a soldier killed in the First Cavalry.

November 2

Nathan had another good day at practice. He didn't have any mistakes that he remembered. Coach Niblett told him he did a good job. Nathan did not feel good about the play in which he only moved his man one yard.

November 3

Renay, a counselor, said that she is seeing more people in counseling now than she ever before. She is caught up with all her paperwork, which takes up a lot of her time. She is praying that God will answer her November prayer and send me home. Renay is going to check to see if WKLD is going to broadcast the game. I preach this Sunday at the main chapel. If Oneonta wins tomorrow, they could end up as state champs. Adam Vinson is still hurt, but the doctor said he might get to play. If not, Colby Tipton will play in his place.

November 4

A lot of people are sending me cards. Renay told me that those people who are writing to me will stand with her and cry tears for me. They want to put their arms around her and pray for me. They are sincerely trying to pull us through this the only way they know how. There have not been any mortar attacks in the last two days. Seems like everything is getting ready for the big attack in Fallujah.

November 5

The Moody game was the roughest game Nathan ever played. One of the Moody players tried to gouge his eye out during the game. Nathan had to develop a street fighting mentality. That is the state of mind that it takes to play football. Coach Niblett frequently said that if he went into a street fight he would want these guys with him. Nathan was committed to the fight and wanted to do his part.

The football team had a nickname for Nathan. They called him "Nasty Nate." Coach Gardner remarked "when Nathan puts on those pads he likes to get a little nasty." Nathan just did not get there on his own; he had to be coached into the football mentality. You could easily see Nathan's laid back disposition and miss his quiet resolve. A sense of purpose is what directs him. His purpose is to live for Christ and be the best he can possibly be in everything he pursues. The players on the team discovered this about Nathan and voted to give him the Christian award his junior and senior years. As chaplain of the Fellowship of Christian Athletes his last two years in high school, Nathan had a weekly opportunity to encourage players on the team to focus on their relationship with Jesus Christ.

Nathan hurt his other shoulder when he knocked the Moody player to the ground.following one of these eye gouging plays.   Now Nathan is going to have to wear braces for both shoulders. I told him to make the season last until Christmas. They have five games left if Oneonta stays in the playoffs. Nathan said that the season will last until December 9, the date of the state championship game. I ask Nathan if he realized before the Moody game started that he would play the most physical game all season. All he needs to do is keep it up, and they can win the state championship. Nathan said that he tried to get spiritually prepared before the game, but he did not know what would happen. Nathan asked God for His will to be done. Nathan said, "I did not think that we had great focus before the game, but we won." I told Nathan that because he is a senior, he needs to speak up to help his team. The devotions he gives at Fellowship of Christian Athletes are important right now.

Renay heard on MSN that the Marines are getting ready to go into Fallujah. She wanted to know if I would be involved in any deaths or injuries that occur there. The U.S. has established a hospital on the outskirts of the city. Renay said there is a lot on TV about Fallujah, so it won't be long before we go in.

November 7
One of the female soldiers in our battalion was wounded by an IED today. She is with the 410th MP Company and a gunner in one of the humvees. She comes to my Bible study a lot. I had prayer with her at the troop medical clinic. She was crying, saying it hurt really bad. It was strange to see wounded soldiers taken on stretchers to a helicopter and flown over to the CSH in the Green Zone.

I preached today at the main chapel. Mathews preached tonight in our chapel. He did a good job. Some of the insurgents in Fallujah have left to go to other cities to cause trouble. It may worsen here now. Renay said, "We will all pray the next few days and weeks."

November 9
There have been machine gun fire and mortar attacks today. Things have calmed down tonight though. Nathan got a shoulder brace he likes. It's just like the one Joe Willie wears. Nathan tells me the story of the Moody player who tried to gouge his eye out twice. The first time Nathan jumped up and yelled to both teams, "This guy is trying to poke my eyes out!" When the player did it again, Nathan spoke to the referee. But when the ref didn't do anything about it,

Nathan slammed the player to the ground. That stopped him.

November 11

The insurgents are on the run. I think they may not be able to group together as they did in Fallujah. In some ways things have gotten worse. Jeanette Statham and the WMU ladies have collected over $2,000 worth of phone cards and are sending them. The Philadelphia Baptist Church has collected $160 for the phone cards. The Fellowship Baptist Church has sent two to three boxes for the troops. Renay has not given up on my being home for the playoffs and the championship game.

Reed, Matthews, "Luckie" and Dennis;
Our chapel choir

Conducting a worship service in Grace Chapel,
Camp Falcon, Baghdad

Coach Niblett and Nathan after practice

Chapter Five
THE SEASON
THAT LASTS FOREVER

November 12

Just had a rocket attack. When the rocket hit I thought someone upstairs had dropped something, but then I heard soldiers running up and down the hall. Soldiers don't run unless something has happened. The rocket hit our headquarters building which is next to the building I am in. I went outside.

I wondered how bad it was and if they were about to pull dead bodies out. How many were dead? What were their names? I learned they had gotten the person out of the room where the rocket hit. I thought to myself, "I'm standing at the foot of the World Trade Center today," as I saw the smoke and flames pour out of the building. Fortunately, only one person was injured. I had to go over to the troop medical clinic to see the wounded soldier. His eye was injured, so they flew him out to the Green Zone. He won't stay there long before they send him to Germany.

This soldier is from my unit, the 231st MP Battalion, his name is Antonio Whetstone and he's only 18 years old. Renay sent out letters to the prayer warriors, and they are praying. Thank God for their prayers on a day like today. Chief Mathews was right above the room where the rocket hit. He was not hurt. He stayed in my room that night due to smoke damage in his room from the attack. The whole unit had to clean all the walls because they were blackened by the resulting fire in Whetstone's room. I got up at 3 a.m. Saturday morning to listen to the Oneonta game over the internet but Mathews slept right through it because I used my head phones. Oneonta beat Dadeville 27-7. Prayer is protection. Because of the number of prayer warriors, Renay said I must be the most prayed for soldier in Iraq.

November 13

Nathan is watching the tape of the Moody game again. Renay said it was his hardest fought game and that he did really well. I'm really having a hard time not being able to see Nathan play. Nathan and Renay are feeling the same way. Renay said that he is trying to do something really hard, like football, without help. We have to be faithful to God, keep trusting Him, and see what He wants to do.

November 14

Talked to Nathan a lot. I asked him to be sure to get the oil changed on the truck. Nathan said that Adam Vincent got to play the first half on defense and then came out for the second half. I preached tonight on Ezekial and the valley of dry bones. Oneonta will play Straughn this Friday. I told Nathan that if Oneonta will run the ball up the middle, they will win the State Championship.

The commander called a morale boosting meeting with the whole battalion after the rocket attack. It will help the unit stay focused and commend them for the good job they are doing. I spoke to the unit, trying to give them something of substance on which to hang their hat. I spoke about how to have the proper perspective and how to deal with stress. Renay mentioned that I had lived in a chaotic situation before—as a child without Christ—and now with Christ. She said, "You know what a difference Christ can make in a situation like this."

November 16

Have been watching the tape of Oneonta's October 15th game with Sumiton Christian. They put all 11 players on the line of scrimmage. Coach Niblett has been teaching the line new blocking schemes, and they have been doing a great job. Renay said that she took Erin and Nathan to see a movie and out to eat to celebrate 11 wins. Oneonta is seeing defenses they have never seen before. Because they are ranked number two, teams are throwing the book at them. Renay said that Nathan is sitting in class all day praying for us and I told her that he needs to quit worrying and be a kid. She told him to keep driving his feet and quit falling down so much during plays. He needs to concentrate every play.

November 17

There are several civilian Iraqi Police Advisors (IPA) living in the building with me. They were leaving the FOB when they stopped to load their weapons. Due to the number of guns and bullets around, weapon discipline should be taken seriously. When one of the passengers opened the back door of the vehicle and reached for his weapon, he accidentally bumped a weapon that was laying underneath his own. When he did so, the weapon fell to the floor of the vehicle, discharged, and killed the driver, Mike Tatar. The other IPAs asked me to conduct his memorial service in our chapel. Mike, was from Denison, Texas. was very friendly. He was very much liked by all who knew him and many attended the memorial service. Chief Mathews was a big help as usual. Major Compton said I did a good job, which is always helpful to me.

November 19

Renay said that our neighbor, Mrs. Jackson, called her to tell me happy birthday on the 21st. Renay said my old unit in Oneonta may be leaving for Afghanistan by December. They keep saying NATO is going to train more of the Iraqi Army. Who knows? We are not doing the same things as when we got here. Far from it, actually. The 127th MP Company out of Germany is doing most of that now. We don't have operational control over them, but we still work with them. Renay wants to know what I want for my birthday. She said that will be the first celebration we have when I get home. Presents will be waiting for me. I'm trying to restore an old truck and want to buy some things for it.

Oneonta is playing Straughn in the playoffs this week. They said they are going to bring a storm over Oneonta. Coach Niblett said at the Quarterback Club that Jesus calmed the storm. He said that they're going to send that storm back where it came from. Renay said that Oneonta is ready to play. She told me to pray for Nathan to drive his feet. It's really hard for me not to be there for these playoff games. Renay says, "Let me tell you that God hears your prayers right there in Baghdad more than mine here in Oneonta. You are doing a lot more for Nathan in prayer than I ever could."

Oneonta beat Straughn 21 to 0 because they ran the ball up the middle. Nathan said that Straughn believed that Oneonta was playing finesse football. He also said he was able to keep his feet better. I told him that I heard the radio announcers compliment the line. Oneonta held Straughn twice on the 1-yard line. Coach Niblett remarked that God helped them do that. It was a miracle. They blitzed a lot, but Coach Niblett had gotten them ready. Nathan agreed. Smash-mouth football always wins.

Luckie, one of our female soldiers, just came by to borrow the cell phone. Luckie is good friends with Whetstone, who is in Germany now recovering from the rocket attack. PV2 Charmelle Luckie, PFC Coylene Reed, and SPC Jennifer Dennis are good friends and provide music as a trio in our chapel services. Chief Mathews leads them. They are a good source for snacks when I need them. I sit in my room while they practice in the chapel. I enjoy hearing them sing. Sometimes I pester them during practice, but not too often because I know Chief Mathews takes his practice time seriously. I sit in on the group's devotion time because I enjoy hearing Mathews speak. I asked him to make his devotions longer because I wanted to hear more.

Oneonta will have to play Pike County. A lot of people will go to Pike County to see the game. After being so hot all summer, it is actually getting cold here in Baghdad.

November 20

Today, I visited three different locations outside the FOB: a base near Sadr City to visit a wounded soldier, the Green Zone to the CSH to visit an Iraqi Police Chief who escaped assassination, and another base to visit a soldier who was hurt in an accident when their vehicle overturned. I prayed and read scripture with the soldiers.

November 21

Today is my birthday. I told Nathan that the game this week will be very physical with lots of blitzes and submarines. They are going to throw their ears back and come at him. Nathan said that Kermit Kendrick sent him a card of encouragement. Somehow he knew I was here in Iraq, and wanted to encourage him. I told Nathan to save it because he was a good player at Alabama.

Spc. Luckie helped me divide the phone cards sent by the WMU, Jeanette Statham, and Neena O'Neal, the pastor's wife at Blountsville Baptist.

November 23

Renay heard on the news that they have trained more troops at Ft. Benning and are headed to Iraq. I wonder if there is any way I could get home to see the state championship game—if Oneonta gets that far. Oneonta will play Pike County this week. They have gotten a lot better in the playoffs. I just told Nathan to play mean and aggressive. Renay told me that the Alabama Baptist State Convention passed a resolution on behalf of chaplains from the state who are serving in combat.

November 25

Thanksgiving Day. Huge Thanksgiving feast at the mess hall. All the food you could eat and of every variety. They try to make it like home. Renay bought Thanksgiving meals for she and the kids and they ate around the computer so we could see each other and talk. Nathan leaves with the team at 1:00 p.m. to go to Brundige to play Pike County. I told Nathan, " You're ready. Beat the snot out of them. Happy Thanksgiving."

November 26

Oneonta beat Pike County 18 to 13—a huge win for Oneonta. Before the game Coach Niblett asked Nathan to gather the offense to pray after each offensive series on the sidelines. Nathan did that. In her prayer warrior letter, Renay writes:

Thank you for praying for the Oneonta Redskins. We were able to brace Nathan's shoulder and he and the other players are staying pretty healthy now. THE ONEONTA REDSKINS ARE 13-0 AFTER A WIN OVER PIKE COUNTY LAST NIGHT! Ernie was able to listen over the internet to the game except for a 10 minute break in the broadcasting in the 4th quarter when Oneonta intercepted a pass. Pike County beat Oneonta last year for the 3A Championship at Legion Field. At the half the score was Pike County 13; Oneonta 12. Ernie said he went into the chapel annex which is across the hall from his room and got on his knees and prayed for the Redskins. None of us wanted to see the Redskin season end like that last night. We knew that God would have to help these boys if they were going to be able to win and if He willed it. Coach Niblett continues to give God the honor and glory for this team. God has His hand on this team. Please pray for our parents and fans that we too would experience what God is doing on this team through the lives of these boys and coaches. Pray for Nathan - there is nothing he wants more than for his teammates to come to know Christ and for his dad to see him play in these playoffs. Oneonta beat Pike County 18-13. Look up Oneonta!

November 27

I ask Nathan what made the difference in the Pike County game. He said Coach Niblett told them to be committed in the second half. They could have easily let the game get out of hand. Pike County is fast and played with a lot of heart. They scored on the first play. Nathan led the offense in prayer about eight or nine times. He said that with a minute left to go in the game, they had to get a first down to wind the clock down. On third and three, Coach Niblett called ISO left behind Nathan. It was up the middle behind Nathan, and they go the first down. The winner of the T.R. Miller vs. Oneonta game will probably be the state champion. T.R. Miller has won six state championships. Oneonta has one. Renay said that we can't look at the past and always know what God is doing in the present. The past can help because it can teach you some things. But living in the moment is the key. We should focus on what God is doing now.

November 28

Tonight I started working on my Christmas messages. Talked to Renay about the packages and cards I've received. Renay said every card and package comes with a prayer. We are thankful for those prayers. I wish I could be home for the last two games of the season. There are things we have to ask God, and if it is His will, it will happen. I talked to Nathan about the upcoming game against T.R. Miller. Oneonta has to score first, fast, and often. The defense has to keep T.R. from scoring. The offense has to keep the ball most of the game and has to put points on the board. Based on T.R. Miller's performance against Midfield, it is possible. T.R. Miller did not score in the second half. It's all about playing hard and praying.

November 29

Coach Niblett is a very stern coach, but believes in players mutually supporting one another. Coach Niblett inherited players who would not speak to each other in the hallways of the school. Over time, Coach Niblett would instruct each player to tell at least three other players that they loved each other and then they would be dismissed to the locker room and take their pads off. It was not uncommon to see the soon to be championship team standing on the sidelines holding hands. Championship leadership would emerge.

Nathan did not feel good about his practice today. Some of the coaches made negative comments. He was upset that he didn't get good movement on some of his blocks. One of the coaches said, "Carroll, if you do junk like that you will get beat every time." Renay said the boys on the team have led the way in getting things right with God. Coach Gilliland got onto Nathan a couple of times, but when he made a good kick out block, Gilliland patted him on the helmet.

November 30

"Prepare your mind for action." 1 Peter 1:13, NIV. I have said on many occasions that I don't see how a person can come to a combat zone and not be right with God. The only thing getting me through this deployment is prayer, faith, and trust in God. The only reward I need is the knowledge that

I fulfilled my military obligation and served God faithfully and honorably. I am just trying to be faithful to God and let what He wants to accomplish through me bring honor and glory to Him. God will help. This is the best center of gravity you can ever have. Faith in God will give an abundance of strength.

December 3

In today's game, T.R. Miller kicked off to Oneonta who drove down the field only to fumble on the T.R. Miller 5-yard line. But they got the ball back, drove down the field, and scored on a Cornelius-to-Bender TD pass from the T.R. Miller 6-yard line. With 2:11 to play in the first quarter, OHS led 6 to 0. Oneonta's Lucas Coffey scored on a 37-yard pass reception from Brody Cornelius. Oneonta kicked off to T.R Miller. The defense held and forced T. R. Miller to punt, but OHS fumbled at the Miller 4-yard line. T.R. Miller missed a field goal attempt right before the half. In the third quarter, TRM was stopped cold on a sack by Tyler Bird. OHS was intercepted at the 4-yard line. Oneonta scored their final touchdown with 5:17 to play in the game. Oneonta led 21 to 0. T.R. Miller eventually scored twice after that, but Oneonta had the victory. I rejoiced with Coach Niblett by cell phone as he and the team were celebrating on the field after the game.[26] Doug and Charlene Smith, great friends and Oneota fans, sat with Renay at the game. Doug leaves a message on the answering machine at home for Nathan after every game telling him what a great job he is doing. He is a great source of encouragement for Nathan.

December 5

I told Nathan that if he wins the state championship, it will be the season that lasts forever. Every play is a championship play. I'm going to visit the guys in the maintenance shop today. They like to gripe, but it's fun just to talk to them and drink coffee. I never know what they will say. The news is saying that recruiting is down. The National Guard is bearing a lot of responsibility for this war.

December 6

Renay has contacted congressmen, the governor's office, the Family Support Advocate, and the State Military Department about the possibility of my coming home to see Nathan play in the state championship game. The request fell on deaf ears. The Adjunct General of the Alabama Army National

---

[26]This analysis based on review of Video Tape, Alpine Advertising.

Guard called Renay to tell her I would not be coming home for the game and that he might go to the game in my place. Renay called Joe Bob Mizzell, Alabama Baptist State Convention, Chaplaincy program who had helped Renay place calls and told him that we will accept that this is God's will. Nathan is playing with a broken heart. He knows now I won't be at the state championship game. People have offered to take up money to fly me home so that I could see the game. They are moved by Nathan's and my commitments to do what we have to do. Renay said, "It is like you are the chaplain of the team by your presence in Baghdad. They are motivated by what you are sacrificing there in not being home for the games. They are motivated to keep going themselves." Renay said they will pray for me to be home for the football banquet in January, and for us to be able to experience the whole season together then. I just want the championship. It will be the season that lasts forever. Because the altar is where the prophets would go to hear a word from the Lord, I have placed the team roster on the pulpit with the cross looking down on it. We need to hear God speak to us and understand what He is saying.

December 7

Nathan had his last practice in pads today. He said he went hard on every play because he knew it was his last. Coach yelled because they weren't focused.

It is the eve of Nathan's championship game. I cannot help but replay in my mind that just last year Nathan was a junior and starting his first varsity game. Thus began Nathan's first year of varsity football as a starter for the Oneonta Redskin football team. The referees penalized Nathan often in those first few games as a starter. A lot of this came from the lack of rhythm yet to develop from playing time. The running backs for Oneonta could have scored several more touchdowns, but the penalties abounded and Nathan got his share. The Cleveland game Nathan's junior year is the first game he started in as a varsity player. The crowd gathered on a hot August evening—the first Friday night of the season. The heat was a factor and to help prevent heat injuries the referees stopped play so the players could take heat time outs.

The first year Coach Niblett was at Oneonta, the Redskins lost to Cleveland by two points. Coach Niblett did not have anyone who could kick extra points. He tried several people to no avail. I kept thinking to myself, as I saw David Barnett down on Nathan's JV team kicking extra points consistently that Coach Niblett sure could use David's ability. Finally, someone must have put a bug in Coach Niblett's ear and told him about David. Before long, Coach Niblett beat a path to David's door to ask him to kick for the varsity.

The question of the day was not if Miguel Hurtado, the junior 5'6" powerhouse would score against Cleveland, but how often. The parents, the band, and all the cheerleaders were eagerly making their way into the stadium as I leaned on the sideline fence to get a good look at Nathan as he warmed up. Nathan's strong suit was his stout legs. He looked powerful in his uniform. Though I knew Nathan might not be the strongest person on the team, he easily compensated with the strength of his legs. Even though Nathan started every game his junior and senior year, I was nervous until I heard the announcer call his name over the loud speaker. Only then did I breathe a sigh of relief.

Nathan did a good job in his first start at left guard for Oneonta. The Redskins won 21 to 0. Oneonta could have scored more—but there were quite a few penalties for holding and blocking in the back or illegal motion. Some of those penalties were Nathan's. Nathan just needed a little more experience.

The second game of the year was against Litchfield. Oneonta knew this was going to be a tough game and it was. The Litchfield crowd was noisy and excited, and the band added to the home field advantage Litchfield already enjoyed. Oneonta did not play well until the second half and ended up losing the game.

The next week in practice Coach Niblett swapped everyone along the line of scrimmage. No one lost their position; they just had to move to another spot on the offensive line, except for Adam Vincent and Nathan. Nathan survived that game by not being demoted to second string or being swapped along the offensive line. This was a positive outcome for Nathan. He had survived that game intact while maintaining his starting position, but there was still room for improvement. Litchfield won 31 to 14.

The Plainview game was another matter. It was the game of the week on a Gadsden radio station. The game was played in Oneonta, and all indications were that it was going to be close. Everyone was impressed with this Plainview team.

As the crowd arrived early for a good seat, the fans were in for a real treat. A nervous excitement filled the air. Our anxiety would turn to jubilation in a matter of minutes. The game captains met in the middle of the field for the coin toss and Oneonta elected to receive. Both teams lined up for the start of the game. Plainview advanced on the ball and kicked to Oneonta. The ball floated down to David Moody who ran the kickoff back for a touchdown. As if that wasn't excitement enough, Oneonta kicked off to Plainview and forced them to punt the ball after Plainview failed to make a first down. Senior Zack Miller ran the ball back for a touchdown, and Oneonta was ahead by two touchdowns before the offense ever stepped foot on the field.

It was a great game. I was excited to see Nathan start on a team that beat Plainview 35 to 14. The fans were jubilant about the potential of this team. The film study on Sunday afternoon was a disaster. That's when it started getting rough for Nathan. The coaches really started jumping on him. He was not going to get a passing score for any of the blocking he did against Plainview.

I remember that my excitement for Nathan was short lived. Nathan came home upset after the next day's practice. That afternoon I remember watching him rotating in and out with a senior. We chewed football during supper and into the evening as we discussed what had happened at practice. I remember asking,

"What's going on Nathan?"

"Coach Niblett said I wasn't playing aggressive enough, so he's swapping me out with other players." Nathan's concern was visible.

"Don't worry about it. Niblett is only trying to fire you up."

While that would ordinarily calm Nathan, this time it was different. I could tell that he felt that he was in a crisis. Nathan had enjoyed starting on the JV team. The prospect of losing his varsity starting position was more than Nathan could take. He was on an emotional rollercoaster and desperately wanted off.

"Coach Gilliland has been telling me I'm leaning."

"What does he mean by that? I see you firing off the ball and you're not letting anyone past you."

"I'm not sure," Nathan said with frustration.

"Well, let's just pray about it and see what the Lord reveals to us," I said as calmly as I could.

That night Renay and I talked until late in the night. We prayed about it and by the next morning after breakfast, I realized what I needed to say to Nathan. After talking to Renay, I knew I needed to go to the school to share what I believed the Lord had led me to tell Nathan.

If Nathan wanted to succeed in football, he would have to take the initiative to ask Coach Niblett what he was doing wrong. Coach Niblett was always willing to help players become the best they could be.

After telling Nathan what I thought, I could see his confidence building. I told Nathan to maintain eye contact with his coach to let him know he was serious. I know Coach Niblett was as focused as a drill sergeant and would respond well. I then told Nathan that I would be praying for him.

I met Nathan at the field house before practice so I could find out what happened. He looked like he felt better and said, "I went into coach's office told him that I wanted to come over to his house to sit down and review the film and let him tell me what I'm doing wrong. Coach Niblett replied that it was my footwork. He said I'm not driving my feet and getting good movement off the line of scrimmage. I'm leaning. He told me what he meant by 'leaning' and then said to make sure that the defensive player never gets passed me on pass pro and to make sure he always stays in front of me."

Somewhat surprised by this positive response, Nathan elaborated more by telling me that Coach Niblett said he was really glad I came to him. It was exactly what he wanted me to do. The results of that conversation made an immediate impact on Nathan. That afternoon at practice I could tell Nathan was really hustling. I will say that I saw Nathan driving his feet faster, harder than he did on JV. To me, Nathan started blocking like an all-pro lineman, not stopping until the whistle blew! It seemed he was now blocking like a man with a mission—a state championship. That goal was achievable, but would require hard work.

Nathan continued to improve as the season progressed. The state championship grew ever closer and the fans could almost taste it.

The "Redskin Moms" emerged this season and began making up their own cheers in the stands. The cheerleaders seemed to love it. These were moms of mostly junior players at the time who ordered T-shirts and sweatshirts each with a different letter spelled on the front and back of their shirts to make the name "R-E-D-S-K-I-N-S." If you saw them as a group from the front or back, you were reminded of the Redskins. But more important than their appearance in the stands was their cheering. Jessie Burton's mom could sport the best war cry followed by cheers of "Do it again! Do it again! We like it! We like it!"

The moms of senior players had their own distinction as "praying moms." You would see them gather before the game and at half time, praying for the safety of the team and for God's will in the game. They met throughout the week as a prayer group and prayed for their sons, the team, and the coaches. On the night before the game, the praying moms would gather on the Redskin 50-yard line on the football field at the stadium. Wrapped in blankets because of the cold and illuminated by flashlights and lanterns, they would pray. Moms even stood in mud on the field from the rain. The spirit of this team community would forever make a lasting impact on the city of Oneonta and Blount County.

When Coach Niblett first came to Oneonta as football coach, he took over a program that had only won one game the previous year and went three and seven the year before that. It was as if the reason the football program existed was for the sole purpose of the band getting on the field to perform at half time. To David Bearden's credit, the band was more renown than the football team. The football fans always felt like they got their money's worth when they came to the games, regardless of the outcome because the band was so good.

Coach Niblett had an off-season conditioning program that would be the envy of other schools. The summer workouts are even more intense than the ones during the school year. Several players have quit the team just because of these workouts. They are gut wrenching. I had never heard of players throwing up because of weight training, but they do in Coach Niblett's program. His program not only involves weight training but speed training also. Coach Niblett could make a turtle run fast. He'll develop fast twitch muscles that a turtle never thought he had. There are teams that have as their goal just to get to the playoffs. Even if they lose the first round playoff game, they consider that success. By the time most schools get to the playoffs, the players are ready to quit and play basketball. Teams that want the state championship are going to capitalize on this and make a run for the championship. Every win in the playoffs is like getting an extra week of spring training practice because the practices can be more intense. The longer you stay in the playoffs the more practice you get under your belt for the following year. Most players want to practice harder for the playoff games. My theory is that a lot of them have been on the scout team all season with little playing time and are trying to make a statement that they are ready to get some game time under their belt. Nathan would have to step it up himself just to keep his position.

The playoffs are played at a different level. The teams play above themselves like you are watching small colleges compete. If you don't get to the playoffs, it's a long time to the next season. Teams that lose one or two games in the regular season can take on a completely different aura for the playoffs and make a legitimate run for the state championship. That's the team you really have to watch out for, because they are often playing with more heart than many of the other teams and that's what wins championships. Playing with heart and character.

Coaches try to add those special touches to the playoffs. They will charter buses to the games instead riding on the yellow school buses. For away games, the serious minded teams will travel to the opponent's home town and stay in a motel overnight and have dinner at the local restaurant. This is done to give the players a feel for the opposing team's home town so it won't feel so much like an away game.

By the time Nathan and the team played in the state championship game in 2003 and 2004, they had played in 30 varsity games in two years. Technically, one game was forfeited to Oneonta in 2004. That is a lot of practice for a high school compared to the 10 regular season games you play if you don't make it to the playoffs.

I was talking to Nathan recently about all these pointers that I had been trying to give him over the past few years and how he put it all together for himself. He described it best when he said, "I had to play with reckless quickness."

"What do you mean?" I said.

Nathan responded, "I had to make sure the lineman stayed right in front of me on pass plays and could not let him get past me." All the while Nathan is saying this he is looking from side to side to see that no one was getting past him. Then on the run plays Nathan said, "I had to make sure that the opposing player was being blocked from here to there." Nathan points to an area about three feet in front of himself indicating that he had to make the opposing player give up ground to him and therefore the running back.

Coaching, teaching, and playing experience aided by prayer, made for skillful interpretation of Nathan's adversary. Nathan quickly sized up his opponents. The more Nathan understood football, the more he came to love the game. Nathan summed it up best when he said, "I didn't pray to win, I played football to win. I prayed that I would play to the glory of God by being the best football player that I could be." He knew that whether the team won or lost that God would get the glory. Coach Niblett would take the loss to build the boys' character and make them better football players and he would take the win for the glory of God. Nathan and I call this approach to football "faith football".

One summer our family was planning a vacation and Nathan needed just one more free day off from workouts. I decided to go to Coach Niblett to see if he would let Nathan take a day off. He said, "We have set a program here whereby, if I let one off I have to let everybody off as well. Nathan could just do up downs to make up for the missed workouts." I said, "Nathan is too conscientious to do that."

I just stated praying for Coach Niblett that somehow a way would work out for our family to take the time we needed for this vacation in a way that Nathan would not be penalized. A few days later, Nathan came home and said that they were given one more makeup day and this would be the extra day we needed for our vacation. That's the way God works in Coach Niblett's life. Everything that needed to work out for Nathan in his relationship with Coach Niblett did because he is a spiritually minded man and listens to God.

One of the things you learn about Coach Niblett early on is that he has a calling to share God's love and it is evident in his work with young people.

When Coach Niblett began his tenure at Oneonta High School he began film study on Sunday afternoon. As a minister this bothered me because I certainly believe that time on Sunday ought to be given to rest and worship. The more I came to understand Coach Niblett and see his love for the Lord, I began to see that his philosophy of coaching is that he sees himself as a life coach of his team. Coach Niblett began teaching a Bible study on Wednesday nights at his home during Nathan's sophomore year. There have been 31 professions of faith in these "Men of Will" Bible Studies. These young men have given their heart and life to Christ and have become active in their local church.

Film study for the week begins on Sunday. Players were to take tapes home and study their position during the week. They were to resume film study on Mondays and Tuesdays at 6:30 a.m. at the field house before school. Wednesday mornings were off as the players were encouraged to attend FCA meetings before school. Often Gail Cornelius and the Spirit Committee would coordinate parents bringing food to these Sunday afternoon studies. Parents would be waiting in the field house and cheer each player as he walked in. Usually a brief speech followed by the coach then we were dismissed for the team to get to work.

Nathan said that Coach Niblett has perfect timing as well. I asked Nathan about that. He said, "On the night before two-a-days at the University of West Alabama, Coach Niblett was leading a Bible study. At the end of his devotion he told the team, "What better time to get saved than before the start of two-a-days." Two-a-days in Niblett's program is grueling.

Oneonta went on to enjoy a great season Nathan's junior year. Oneonta beat Colbert County 15-0 in the fourth round of the playoffs to advance to the championship game. This win earned the Redskins a spot in the state championship against Pike County.

Thanks to an amazing quarterback, Pike County won 30-7. With the taste of greatness in their mouths, the team would not be satisfied until they took the trophy home. Nathan's junior year Oneonta beat teams in the northern region; this year Oneonta is beating every team in the southern region they have played. Only one team stood between Oneonta and the championship game - TR Miller. Coach Niblett's goal was not to be a runner up again this year. His goal is the championship.

December 9

Today is the day of the State Championship game. The game is played at Legion Field in Birmingham- The Old Gray Lady. In order to hear it played at 3:00 p.m. Birmingham time, I will have to get up at midnight. I will listen over the internet. I understand that the school put a blue and white Christmas tree in the school lobby. They put a blue ribbon on it that says, "I'm Dreaming of a Blue Trophy Christmas." Renay said that Miguel and several others hit hard at practice. She thought they did this because they want it so bad. Miguel, Adam Vincent, Cameron LaRue, and Nathan were voted team captains for the game. Renay will call by cell phone during the game.

On the first play, Brody Cornelius threw a swing pass to Miguel Hurtado who ran the ball to Oneonta's 39-yard line. Number 4, Dajuan White, thought he could tackle Miguel, but he was wrong. Miguel hit him hard, and White stayed on the ground for a bit. Coach Niblett immediately gathered his players and led them in prayer for White. White got up, shook it off, and played the remainder of the game. After a defensive stop, Oneonta was forced to punt. On the very next play, Winfield did the unthinkable. The quarterback, Blake Franks, faked the handoff, dropped back, and passed to Number 25, who scored on the 61-yard pass play from the Winfield 39-yard line. Winfield was up 7 to 0.

Winfield kicked off to Oneonta, and the teams swapped the ball until Winfield was forced to punt. On a first down play in Oneonta territory, Brody Cornelius handed the ball to Anthony Mostella who fumbled at the 30-yard line. Several plays later, Winfield's Drake Hall scored on a run from the 3-yard line with 55 seconds left on the clock in the first quarter.

After several series with little action, Oneonta managed to get to the Winfield 32-yard line. On the next play, Miguel Hurtado ran between the right guard and tackle on a play where Nathan, the left guard, pulled and kicked out the end coming across the line of scrimmage. Miguel was able to get to the 1-yard line. On fourth down with 1:55 left in the second quarter, Miguel scored on a run on the left side of the line. For the moment, things were looking up for Oneonta.

Winfield took over at their own 31-yard line. Brent Bender kept Winfield from scoring by shoving Drake Hall out of bounds. Oneonta had a great defensive stand. On fourth and goal from the OHS 5-yard line, Winfield's Will Vickery attempted a field goal, but missed. The score remained 14 to 7 Winfield at the half.

I went to the altar in the chapel to pray for Nathan and Oneonta. I thought to myself, "What am I going to say to Nathan if Oneonta loses? At least you got to go back to the championship game again?" That didn't make much sense to me. Then I called Renay to get a feel for the game. She said the fans were beside themselves wondering what was going on. The first half had gone nothing like the first 14 games of the season. Mistakes and penalties were wearing hard on the team, but the fans knew they could come back. Renay was praying they would. She said that Nathan was leading the offensive line in prayer on the sidelines after every series. It seemed that some of the inexperienced players on the team were distracted by the cameras and the awe of playing for a championship trophy at Legion Field. The team would need to focus.

In the second half, Oneonta kicked to Winfield, who was soon forced to punt. Oneonta moved the ball to the Winfield 26-yard line. Miguel shifted to the quarterback position, and the snap sailed over his head back to the 42. The next play, Brody attempted a pass that fell incomplete and Winfield took over at their own 42-yard line. Eleven plays later Winfield scored on a 9-yard run with 40 seconds to go in the third quarter. The score was 21 to 7. On Oneonta's next drive they managed a first down after a 20-yard pass completion. But the drive stalled and with 11:02 left in the fourth quarter. Oneonta faced a fourth and nine. After a time out, Brody Cornelius gathered his troops on the field. From their own 41, Brody Cornelius lined up at quarterback in a shotgun formation with Miguel Hurtado in the back field. Lucas Coffey went in motion to the left crossing in front of Brody, and just as he got past Brody, the ball was snapped. Brody, under pressure, rolled left, then rolled right and took a step to his left. He lofted the ball all the way back across the field to the left where Miguel stood as if he were simply directing traffic on the field. The ball arched its way in Miguel's direction as if it had a mind of its own. Miguel interrupted the ball on its way toward the sideline, quickly grabbed the ball as if he had kidnapped it, and ran down to the 9-yard line. A face mask penalty of half the distance to the goal took the ball down inside the three. On second and goal from the 2-yard line, with 9:52 left in the game, Anthony Mostella scored on a running play on the left side of the offensive line bringing the score to 21 to 14. The offense offered up prayers giving God the glory.

After the kick off, Oneonta put up a defensive stand. Cameron LaRue made a tackle behind the line of scrimmage, and a penalty put the ball at the 12-yard line. On the next play, Winfield's Drake Hall fumbled when Adam Vincent burst through the line of scrimmage to hit him. Nick Ratliff recovered the fumble. Three plays later Miguel Hurtado scored on a screen pass on the left side. With 7:02 left to play in the game, the score was tied.

After a running play and an incomplete pass, Byrd almost sacked the quarterback at the 3-yard line. After a punt, which put the ball on Winfield's 40-yard line, Mostella ran left and gained nine yards. Then he ran to the right and got the first down. On the next play, Brody Cornelius handed the ball to Miguel who hit the line of scrimmage. When he did, Coach Gilliland exclaimed, "He's gone!" Miguel ran the ball on the left side of the line for the touchdown, giving Oneonta the lead with 3:52 left on the clock. But the game was far from over.

After several more series in which neither team scored, the Redskins were forced to punt, but Brody bobbled the snap. Winfield blocked the punt and recovered at Oneonta's 18-yard line. Winfield ran another play, but there was no gain. On the next play, Winfield took the snap, rolled right, and threw the ball to Lee Sims, who promptly ran the intercepted ball out of bounds at Winfield's 48. The game ended two running plays later. Oneonta won 28-21.

Oneonta was State Champion! The Oneonta Redskins gave God the glory for helping them to play to the best of their ability and sought to give Him the honor and glory for "The Perfect Season." After an announcement, the blue trophy was presented, and the celebration began as a torrential downpour of rain flooded the field.[27]

After the trophy was presented, Nathan began making his way off the field. Renay said the look on his face was one of sheer exhaustion and relief. I am reminded of the apostle Paul's words in 2 Timothy 4:7, KJV, "I have fought a good fight, I have finished my course, I have kept the faith." Nathan and Renay met and embraced over the fence, held each other and cried as the rain flooded the field.

The Oneonta Redskins had just won their first state championship in 32 years. After the presentation of the trophy, there were hugs and congratulations all around. When the team arrived back in Oneonta, Renay told me car horns blared and headlights flashed a congratulatory hello. The team stepped off the bus cheering. While they put their gear away in the field house, fans and parents waited quietly for the team to emerge. You could hear only whispers as fans stood in silence, respect, and awe over what had happened. One by one the players filed out of the field house and melted into the fog as they made their way onto the field. Coach Niblett invited the parents and fans to join the team on the field for prayer. They all held hands in a large circle as Coach Niblett thanked God for the championship win. Nathan and the other offensive lineman circled up for their own prayer of thanksgiving and agreed that they would be forever bonded together because of that season and that night.

December 10

In the days following the championship the city of Oneonta would celebrate the championship. Renay told me that for several days after the

---

[27]This analysis based on review of the Video Tape, Alpine Advertising.

game parents and players would hold the Blue Trophy but she never did. She said it didn't seem fair. She would wait for me to hold it first but I never would. The Blue Trophy was securely locked in the school trophy case in the lobby of OHS next to the 1972 state championship trophy earned 32 years earlier.

December 13-14

Today and tomorrow the team turns in their pads. By the time Nathan and the team played in the state championship game in 2003 and 2004, they had played in 30 varsity games in 2 years. The Fultondale game in 2004 was a forfeit. That is a lot of practice for a high school compared to the 10 regular season games you play if you don't make it to the playoffs. Nathan will hang up his pads today. He and the team were given their game day jerseys and we purchased his helmet.

December 17

A parade is held today in honor of the team and Renay said the entire city of Oneonta came to proudly cheer the team and hear the band. After parading down Highway 75 in front of the county courthouse a brief ceremony ensued when the mayor declared this day as the 2004   3A Championship Football Team day. Coach Niblett spoke to the players, parents and fans giving God the glory for the win. He announced money needed to purchase the Championship Rings would be raised. The players would not have to pay any of the cost of the rings.

The team walked from the court house across the street to the First Baptist Church where in their fellowship hall tables lined the walls for the players to sit and sign autographs. Pictures, posters, footballs and t shirts celebrating The Perfect Season were signed. Coach Niblett would autograph a picture to Nathan with the message: "To Nathan, the greatest Christ like player I will ever have coached." To Renay he wrote: "Your strength has been an inspiration to this team."

December 20

The Championship has taken its toll. Christmas is this week and Renay says nothing has been done at home to prepare. Renay had decided not to put up a tree. I called my secretary at the association office and gave her my credit card number asking that she buy a tree and have it delivered with a note attached: "To Erin and Nathan. Love, Dad." Erin and Nathan decorated the tree. Tonight I conducted a special service in my chapel. I invited the choir from the main chapel to come and have a musical celebration of Christmas. I asked Chief Mathews to have our chapel choir sing. There were also soloists that would sing as well. The soldiers were surprised at what a great time they had. I took pictures of all the weapons they placed in my bedroom while they were singing. I couldn't believe all those machine guns and rifles just piled up in the corner.

December 22

I received a Bible in the mail today from Renay and the kids for Christmas. It has my name, 2004, Baghdad, Iraq, printed on the front cover. Renay, Erin and Nathan's presents arrived several days ago back home and they will open my presents for them on Christmas Day.

December 24

Christmas Eve. Renay and I were on the internet. Renay asked and I responded,

"Did you hear the blast in Baghdad?"

"No"

"Just happened"

" I hear noises and don't know what they are."

" An oil truck in western Baghdad exploded."

"What, where, why?"

"In the upscale district in western Baghdad. They are just getting it in on CNN."

"Was it terrorists?"

"Probably"

" Must have attacked a church."

"Said oil truck with explosives."

"That's a big one. How long ago was it?"

" Just happened in the last thirty minutes. Was on CNN in the last 15 minutes."

I then left for a briefing.

December 25

Christmas Day. One of the hardest days in Iraq. Renay wants us to open the presents I sent Erin and Nathan over the internet on web cam. She bought them Christmas dinners from a local restaurant so we could eat our Christmas meal together. Renay did not spend Christmas with her family choosing to spend that time with me over the internet. She, Erin, and Nathan will go to my family's Christmas celebration after our meal together is over and I will go to bed ending the day. The hardest thing in the world is to be sitting in Baghdad watching my family eat Christmas dinner and open presents.

Jack Bains Photography

Giving God all the glory before the game.

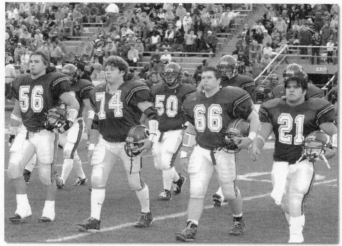

Jack Bains Photography

Team Captains for the State Championship
left to right. Adam Vinson, Cameron Larue,
Nathan Carroll, Miguel Hurtado

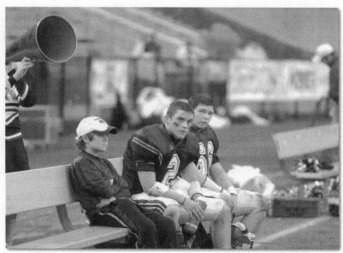

Jack Bains Photography

Brody Cornelius, QB, and Nathan;
Redskins score 2nd quarter, win in sight.

Jack Bains Photography

Champion Coach

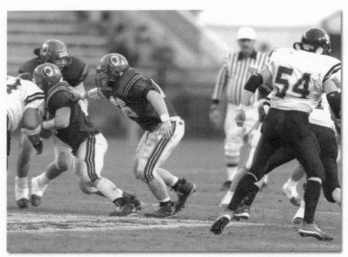

Jack Bains Photography

Putting it all on the line for the Championship.

Chapter Six
THE MAKING OF
FATHERS AND SONS

January 5, 2005

A call came to the 410 TOC (Tactical Operations Center) where I was visiting soldiers that a convoy from the 410 was reporting four Iraqis had waved them down which is cause for danger. The men used hand signals and gestures to warn the soldiers of impending danger. Stopping was risky, but proved to be wise. An interpreter discovered that two people wearing ski masks had planted two boxes, one yellow and one black, with wires hanging out of them on the side of the road. The convoy commander verified that the two boxes were IEDs and immediately set up a security perimeter to block traffic.

The sergeant in charge of the TOC reported that the bomb was set to go off in either eight minutes or at eight o'clock. They were trying to get the bomb squad to the scene and warn others to stay away.

I began praying. Both the gunner in the top of the vehicle and those pulling security outside the vehicle are vulnerable to sniper attacks. In situations with two IEDs, one is sometimes a decoy and one is meant to distract while the other is then set off. This is the way insurgents ambush convoys.

All visitors to the TOC were kept outside in the hall. I prayed that no one would be harmed in any way. One soldier plotted the position of the convoy on the map, while another documented conversations and maintained radio contact. When the eight-minute detonation deadline passed and nothing happened, the bomb squad detonated the bomb.

As we were getting ready for Bible study that night, my chaplain assistant Spc. Harrison, who was returning from his two-week leave, began telling me that on the way back to the FOB they ran into an IED. When I ask him about the circumstances surrounding the event, he described the exact situation I had been praying about. He was in the convoy at the IED site that afternoon I told him of my prayers.

The Lord was really watching over Harrison. God put me in that TOC so I could pray. Prayer is protection. .

January 6

Today is our 27th wedding anniversary. Renay says we will celebrate Christmas, birthdays and the Championship when I get home. When I get home, Renay will have the "Blue Trophy" Christmas tree that stood in the OHS school lobby during the week of the Championship for our tree. Presents will be wrapped under the tree. Nathan says he wants us to take a Championship Road Tour and visit all the game sites where he played, walk on their football fields and try to give me a feel for each win. I cannot tell you how bad this hurts. Renay says, "I wish by taking a bath I could wash this pain off."

I am writing a book. Somehow I want to describe my life "before Baghdad" and "after Baghdad." My family and I will look for a "new normal."

Every day in staff meetings all of us in the unit are looking for dates of when our tour will end. We are hearing of our replacements coming in February but we have no redeployment date announced. My conversations with Renay are always about coming home and when that will happen. She wants me to ask anybody, everybody I know what have they heard. I keep packing, watching to see if the connexes are being moved. I just keep packing. Renay encourages me to ask questions. She says, "Asking questions could relieve some of the pain we carry every second of every minute of every day."

The following is the last letter sent to our Prayer Warriors:

January 2005
Hello from Baghdad and thank you for continuing to pray. Things have been relatively quiet, in a manner of speaking, around the FOB (forward operating base) lately. Since the suicide bombing in Mosul, we have been wearing our body armor whenever we go outside. Body armor is very heavy, but thank goodness it's cool outside this time of year. When we have church services or go to the dining facility (DFAC) we have to show our ID. The security has gotten a lot tighter around here.

Thanks to all who sent Christmas cards and to the WMU groups that sent the phone cards. Thanks to Jenette Statham for all you do. I really appreciate it. The soldiers appreciate it.

We celebrated Christmas as well as you can when away from family in a foreign country. I invited the Protestant service praise team, the gospel service choir, and our own chapel trio for a Christmas Fest at our chapel annex. The choirs were surprised to have had such a good time.

Words can't begin to tell you how badly I missed being home for the big game. Nathan, ever a faithful witness, was God's man on the team this year. God blessed him for his faithfulness. Many times during a game I had to get on my knees at the altar to pray. I plan to really celebrate when I get home.

Yesterday I attended a memorial service for a soldier killed in a vehicle accident. These vehicles are not built with safety in mind. It takes so little for them to be knocked off the road. From what I've seen, even though they are armored they can't absorb a lot of impact and are knocked over easily. One of the other soldiers involved in the accident made a profession of faith and was baptized this past Sunday at the main chapel on post.

I have been on active duty now for over a year and am in my tenth month here in Baghdad. We have had some other companies move up under us, so our battalion is now the largest in Baghdad.

The redeployment date is sometime in March. Don't know anything for certain. On Wednesday nights, I teach Bible study in the book of Joel—the third major prophet we've studied. It is interesting to study the Bible in a land that was the setting for so many biblical events. I've learned that the prophets often received their prophecy at the altar and would share God's word with the congregation. That really spoke to me. Now we have a prayer box on the pulpit. No one sees the prayer requests, and each person that places a prayer request in the box is encouraged to pray at the altar. I think we should really encourage our congregations to go to church during the week, not just on Sunday and Wednesday night, to pray at the altar.

God Bless, Ernie

January 8

Today is the football sports banquet honoring the accomplishments of the team and the awarding of individual awards. Hundreds of players family members, fans and students attend this coat and tie event each year. Erin and Renay will be there for Nathan. Renay will video the event for me so I can experience it when I get home.

The only event I may be able to experience with Nathan and the team is the awarding of the Championship ring sometime in early March when the rings are finished. Nathan has always dreamed of this ring. He refused to buy a high school ring in the spring of his junior year because he said, "How would I wear it if I am going to wear my Championship ring on the same finger." He knew his junior year before ever going and ultimately winning the Championship game his junior and senior year that one day, God willing, he would own the high school 3A State Championship ring. Nathan has asked Coach Niblett to place diamond chips in the ring and Coach has agreed.

January 9

Nathan told me he was awarded the Most Improved Lineman award and the Christian award voted on by the team. Renay says of the banquet, "It was emotional for the Oneonta community because of all the stories like Nathan, and like Jake and Adam having surgery and all Miguel's family has been through."

January 13

I have been told today of the Redeployment Briefings I will conduct for the battalion as we prepare to go home. I will conduct them on February 1 and 3. These briefings are intended to help the soldier transition back into civilian life.

January 20

Renay asks, "What was it that you said on the phone this morning about Nathan had to do it without his dad like you had to do it without your dad? Do what?" I replied, "I had to do what I did without a dad to help and Nathan reached a point in his life that he had to so something without his dad." "Right" Renay replied. "And you know what I think. It was not your fault that Nathan reached that point in his life and it was not your dad's fault that he could not help you do what you have had to do. Neither dads are at fault.

Neither dad was able to change his circumstance." I said, "I do understand my dad better now than I ever have. I have done the same thing he has done. We are both combat veterans."

January 29

Nathan was awarded the All County First Team Offensive trophy voted on by the Blount County Coaches. Coach Niblett was named Coach of the Year. It was a great honor but due to a mix up in times of presentation, Renay and Nathan arrived after the presentation was made for Nathan and the other players. Nathan was obviously disappointed over the web cam but thankful for this honor. Last year he was awarded All County Second Team Offense.

January 30

Renay tells me that the Iraqi elections are a huge success. People are saying that by their voting that they reject the insurgents and thank every American soldier that is there and all who have given their lives.

I asked, "Where did they hear that?"

"All the news people on TV are reporting it that way.

President Bush came on T.V. and said it was rejection of the insurgents."

Went to a briefing today. Redeployment date is set for no later than March 10. Some of the officers are saying they are going to try to move the date up.

February 1

Have been conducting redeploymnet briefings. One of the briefings has been with the unit that has been guarding Saddam Hussein. Went to the building where they are holding him but did not see him.

Having a lot of soldiers coming by to see me for counseling for health and family issues due to the deployment. One soldier made a stupid comment about how to relieve stress and he was made to go back through the redeployment briefings. Had another soldier that came by to try to get home to his children because they had been taken into custody by the court system in his home town because of alleged abuse. I wanted him to go home. The commander wouldn't let him. Soldiers are coming out of the stress of this year long deployment for counseling. I counsel them, many of whom are the age of my children back home, as a father would his children. I refer some of them to the mental health officer to document some of their reporting.

February 2

The TOA (Transfer of Authority) ceremony will be March 6. I will be asked to lead in prayer. The other soldiers in my unit will leave prior to the TOA and I will leave with the commander after this ceremony.

February 3

Hearing of the 504th Military Police Battalion from Fort Lewis, Washington, coming in and every available bed is being used. We will be full at the FOB for the next few weeks as we train our counterparts for their mission. Mission over. Home soon.

February 20

There was some kind of accident this morning and I was called out of the chapel. One company under our battalion had some soldiers going to the firing range for practice, while other soldiers from the same unit had pulled into our FOB for instructions and security. My role was to talk to the soldiers and offer prayer for them and the injured soldiers. I did my best with the small amount of information I had.

These soldiers were part of the personal security detachment for Negraponte, the American Ambassador to Iraq. The route they had taken had extensive IED activity and, as the convoy was traveling down the highway, they had come to an overpass. The drivers are trained to weave as they pass through the area because if there is an IED hanging from underneath the bridge and it explodes, the vehicles following the explosion hopefully will not be in the path of the detonation. Because of the extra armor, the humvee is top heavy and requires extra care in maneuvering. As the lead vehicle made this maneuver, it began to swerve out of control and rolled off the highway. The other vehicles came to a halt and went to the aid of their comrades. As they dismounted their vehicles, they radioed for a helicopter to evacuate the two injured soldiers. With the injured soldiers on stretchers, they were making their way to a waiting helicopter in the highway median. Suddenly, there was an explosion which further injured the already wounded soldier and killed the three soldiers carrying the gurney, 1st Lt. Jason Timmerman, SGT David Day, and SSG Jesse Lhotka. The helicopter was put out of commission and another was called in to evacuate the wounded and the casualties.

As the news spread, pastoral care and consoling turned to grief counseling. I was sent to the American Embassy to minister to the other soldiers in the unit and plan a memorial service for February 25. Their story reminded me of the four friends who carried their sick friend on a stretcher and lowered him down through the roof of the house where Jesus was staying so that Jesus might heal him. These soldiers were doing the same thing for their injured friend.

I recalled the words that Paul spoke in Ephesians 5:2 when he said, "Live a life filled with love, following the example of Christ. He loved us and offered himself as a sacrifice for us, a pleasing aroma to God." (LASB) The same love that Paul was encouraging us to have is the same Christ-like love and concern that Timmerman, Day, and Lhotka had for their fellow soldiers. These men were the embodiment of love.

Lt. Jason Timmerman was a school teacher and a computer tech at an insurance company. He was a very caring, deeply religious person. He was always talking about his family. He had a brother who was studying to become a priest. He always asked the right questions during briefings. He went the extra mile to see that things were the way they should be. He was committed to excellence.

SSG Jesse Lhothka took the time to talk to others. His favorite television program was "Friends" and he always wanted people to watch it with him. Never hard to get along with, he was a people person and a problem solver. He served as a father figure to so many back home—always calling to stay in touch.

SSG David Day was the epitome of care and concern for the soldiers' well being. Short and built like an ox, he had a unique laugh and was extremely nice and easy to talk to. He was a newlywed. He was a buddy to everyone and enjoyed having coffee with guys at the cafeteria.

These three soldiers sacrificed their lives so that the Iraqi people could experience the blessings of freedom. They died to preserve the same freedom for our own country. Incidents like these should remind those back home of the cost of freedom.

In contrast to so many in our culture today, their personal ambitions were not of selfish gain but of service to others. The one word that best describes their service is that of unassuming "heroism." Therefore we owe them the dignity to be indebted to them for the burden they have carried— unconditional regard for people to be free. It was a load of "select service." These men selected military service as an obligation to our country. They were not ordinary citizens. These men were true patriots. America needs more patriots.

March 6

Our unit has left in small groups and are waiting for the commander's staff to join the unit in Kuwait. When we came to Baghdad a year ago, we were flown into the Baghdad airport and convoyed into Baghdad. Now security has tightened and we are flying out in small groups at night by Black Hawk helicopter. Having completed our responsibilities at the TOA ceremony, I will get to the Troop Medical Clinic   in plenty of time to line up for the flight to the Baghdad airport. I am finally on my way home.

March 9

Leaving Baghdad airport for Kuwait today. Mission over. Home soon.

March 10

Only in Kuwait for 24 hours. Flying out today. Will be in Fort Benning after a 12-18 hour flight. Called Renay from Ireland and gave an estimated time of arrival as midnight. Renay and Nathan came to Fort Benning this morning to get room reservations for us. Erin will come from Samford with my sisters, Debra and Sheila, who are coming for the reunion. I am told we will be in Fort Benning for a period of time and then after a brief homecoming ceremony in Prattville, the unit will be dismissed. Renay is trying to delay the Championship ring ceremony until I get home. Rings were to be ready at the beginning of March but they were delayed. I am praying this is a ceremony I will not miss.

Ready to go home for Starnes,
Richardson and me at Baghdad airport.

David Wilson, Blount Photography

The 13 seniors of the 2004
Oneonta Redskin Championship Team

Welcome Home

CONCLUSION

I cannot describe in words my experiences of war in a combat zone for 12 months of my life. The images and feelings—the thoughts and experiences—will forever be etched in my heart and mind. My family will carry their experiences and sacrifices into our future together.

I hope I have provided a glimpse into the role of a chaplain in combat and the sacrifices families are making in the Iraqi Freedom war effort. The most difficult part of my experience was my responsibility to conduct memorial services. Even though I prayed I would not have to conduct even one, I conducted five memorial services for six fallen soldiers and one Iraqi Police Advisor. These soldiers died defending freedom for our country: Spc. Ty Vue, Willows, California; First Lt. Timothy Price, Midlothian, Virginia; Spc. Clifford L. Moxley, New Castle, Pennsylvania; First Lt. Jason Timmerman, Tracy, Minnesota; SSG Jesse Lhothka, Alexandria, Minnesota; SSG David Day, St. Louis Park, Minnesota; and Mike Tatar, IPA, Denison, Texas.

I hope in chronicling the Oneonta Redskin football team's 2004 season, I have relayed the passion and excitement felt by those involved. Memories of that season will last forever in the hearts and minds of the team, their coaches, their parents, and their fans. My experience in Baghdad of that season—through the Internet, e-mails, web cams, instant messaging, and video tapes—is quite different from that of many others. During this difficult time of separation, love found a way to connect us all. Renay, Erin, Nathan and I traveled to Nasssau March 20-24 for a time to reconnect over Spring Break. I was able to attend the Championship ring ceremony on March 29.

God reveals to us that Love found a way to reach sinful man through the death of His Son, Jesus Christ. Love is stronger than death. Through Christ we find the love that produces courage and character. As I have witnessed soldiers on the battlefield, I have seen the courage and character it takes to be a champion. I have had the unique opportunity to work with the finest young people in America—the American soldier. At the same time, I experienced the courage and character of a football team under the leadership of Coach Niblett, who took average young men and turned them into champions on the football field. I have learned that courage is defined by moments. An average person confronted with a defining moment can become a courageous hero.

This book is written for you 13 seniors who helped lead your team to victory.

It is tradition for the Auburn University football team to sing the school's fight song, *War Eagle*, when they win. The 2004 team added another song, *Hard Fighting Soldier* by Allen Coker, to celebrate the victory which cinched the SEC West title. I think it says it well:

I am a hard fighting soldier, on the battlefield
I am a hard fighting soldier, on the battlefield
I am a hard fighting soldier, on the battlefield
I keep on bringin' souls to Jesus
By the service that I give
I've got a helmet on my head, in my hand a sword and shield
I've got a helmet on my head, in my hand a sword and shield
I've got a helmet on my head, in my hand a sword and shield
I keep on bringin' souls to Jesus
By the service that I give
You gotta walk right, talk right, sing right, pray right, on the battlefield
You gotta walk right, talk right, sing right, pray right, on the battlefield
You gotta walk right, talk right, sing right, pray right, on the battlefield
I keep on bringin' souls to Jesus
By the service that I give
I am a hard fighting soldier, on the battlefield
I am a hard fighting soldier, on the battlefield
I am a hard fighting soldier, on the battlefield
I keep on bringin' souls to Jesus
I keep bringin' souls to Jesus
We keep bringin' souls to Jesus
By the service that we give[28]

HOOAH!

---

[28]Song Directory, <u>Hard Fighting Soldier,</u> Acadisc. Co. Jan. 15, 2006,
  >http:// www.acadisc.com/index.htm>

BIBLIOGRAPHY

Bentley, L.D. Sr. WKLD Radio. Broadcast. Oneonta: WKLD. 2004.

Gibbons, Chuck. <u>Football 2004 Sports Banquet Program</u>, Oneonta, Alabama.

McAlpine, Robbie. Alpine Advertising. Videotape. Oneonta: Alpine. 2004.

Nori, Don. <u>The Hope of a Nation that Prays</u>. Shippensburg, Pennsylvania: Destiny Image Inc., 2001.

Song Directory, <u>Hard Fighting Soldier,</u> Acadisc. Co. Jan. 15, 2006, >http:// www.acadisc.com/index.htm>

1466706

Made in the USA